double bass drumming

Joe Franco

Modern Drummer Publisher/CEO **David Frangioni**

President **David Hakim**

Back cover photos by Steve Pace

Published by:
Modern Drummer Media, LLC.
1279 W Palmetto Park Rd
PO Box 276064
Boca Raton, FL 33427

Subscribe to *Modern Drummer*, the world's best drumming magazine, at:
www.moderndrummer.com/subscribe

For fun and educational videos, subscribe to the
"Modern Drummer Official" YouTube channel.

JOE FRANCO   **ABOUT THE AUTHOR**

Born in New York City, Joe started his drumming career playing the club circuit in New York. He recorded six albums and toured constantly with the popular New York band "Good Rats." Since then, Joe has toured and recorded with "Twisted Sister," "Chilliwack," Fiona, Leslie West, Jack Bruce, Vinnie Moore, Blues Saraceno and most recently "Widowmaker." He has also recorded albums with Taylor Dayne, Mariah Carey, Hall and Oates, Celine Dion, Doro Pesch and "Baton Rouge" among others. Besides his album credits, Joe is one of the most in-demand session drummers in New York City, playing on many jingles and soundtracks.

In the educational field, after writing "Double Bass Drumming," Joe recorded an instructional video with the same title (also distributed by CPP/Belwin). He writes many articles for "Modern Drummer" and other drum magazines. Joe is also known for the excellent clinics he conducts for Premier Percussion and the Zildjian Cymbal Co.

INTRODUCTION

Double Bass Drumming was originated by Louie Bellson in the Big Band Era, during the 1940 s. Since that time, the concept of playing two bass drums was uncommon until the late 60 s, with the arrival of Ginger Baker and the Cream. Many Rock drummers of this period began adding a second bass drum. They were joined by a wave of Jazz-Rock Fusion players in the 70 s, as the double drum kit became increasingly popular.

Over the past few years, while performing and conducting clinics. I've been asked many questions in regard to playing two bass drums. This encouraged me to organize my ideas and define a practical method of playing, the foundation of which is presented in this book. Throughout the book, all of the bass drum rhythms are written using a method which I call "The Single Stroke System" This system will enable a drummer to play double bass in a powerful and consistent sounding manner. Powerful, in that all rhythms are played using single strokes and consistent sounding in that they are played in a systematic way.

The three parts of the book were designed with practical application in mind. They should be studied simultaneously. All of the double bass rhythms in Part I are presented with a ride and snare to form what are commonly called "Beats" All of the hand-foot combination patterns in Part II are presented as "Fills" Part III deals with "Soloing over the double bass roll" Each of the three parts have two sections — a sixteenth note section and an eighth note triplet section. The gradual progression within each section will especially help a single bass player adapt to playing two bass drums.

While writing this book, I had the opportunity to teach in the New York Metropolitan area and was happy with the results obtained using this system. This was a learning experience for me; I hope it will be for you! Enjoy.

Joe Franco

A NOTE FROM THE PUBLISHER

Joe Franco's Double Bass Drumming is one of the few true gold-standard books on the art of double bass drumming to quickly, through practice, your playing. Regardless of the style of music that you play, Joe's book will improve your control, speed and overall vocabulary so that you can play the ideas in your head on the kit with your feet!

I've been using Double Bass Drumming for over 30 years, and it always brings me improved results when applied to the music that I'm playing (especially rock drumming). The key is to go through the exercises slowly and practice with heels up and with heels down so that you build all the necessary muscles.

I want to thank Joe Franco for creating this work of art and sharing his knowledge and experience with the world. Joe is an amazing person, and we are proud to call him a friend and collaborator of the Modern Drummer family!

David Frangioni
CEO/Publisher of Modern Drummer Publications, Inc.

DOUBLE BASS DRUMMING

TABLE OF CONTENTS

PERFORMANCE NOTES

Time Signature

All of the musical notation in this book is in 4/4 time The concepts presented can be applied to other time signatures

Code Notation

B D 1, B D.2 see The Single Stroke System page 3
RIDE refers to the ride cymbal, but can be played on any sound source in the drum kit, for example, closed hi hat, cowbell, tom or electronic percussion
HANDS see Part II page 31

Staff Notation

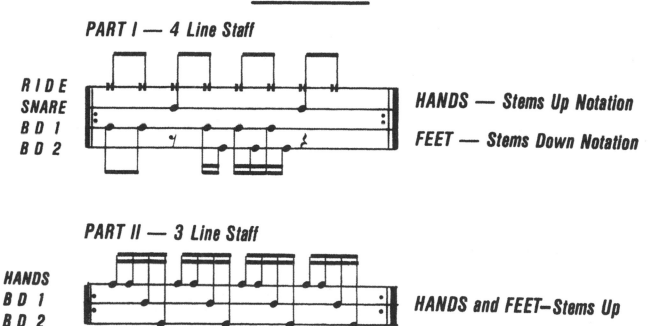

PART I — 4 Line Staff

RIDE
SNARE
B D 1
B D 2

HANDS — Stems Up Notation

FEET — Stems Down Notation

PART II — 3 Line Staff

HANDS
B D 1
B D 2

HANDS and FEET—Stems Up

PART III — Hands On 1 Line Staff — Stems Up
Feet On 2 Line Staff — Stems Down

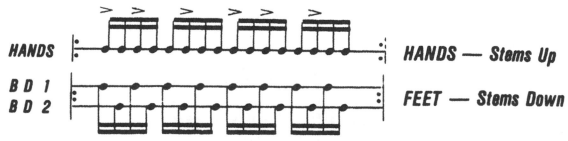

HANDS

B D 1
B D 2

HANDS — Stems Up

FEET — Stems Down

Practicing With A Metronome

I strongly recommend the use of a metronome when practicing A suggested tempo for practicing this book is ♩ = 100 — 120 for all the sixteenth note sections and ♩ = 140 — 160 for all the eighth note triplet sections.

THE SINGLE STROKE SYSTEM

> **Bass Drum Code:**
> B.D.1 refers to the main bass drum
> B.D.2 refers to the second bass drum (on the hi hat side).

Throughout this book B.D.1 and B.D.2 are written in a consistent way using a method which will be referred to as The Single Stroke System. This system is based on the *single stroke* double bass drum roll, led by the main bass drum (B D.1). For example, here is the sixteenth note double bass roll, led by B.D.1:

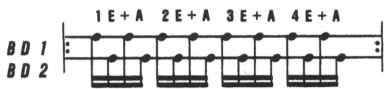

The Single Stroke System is used to break up a rhythmic pattern between two bass drums in the following way:

> A rhythmic pattern is played on B.D.1 and B.D.2 as if the notes of the pattern were part of the single stroke double bass roll.

The following example illustrates how this system is used to break up a sixteenth note pattern between two bass drums:

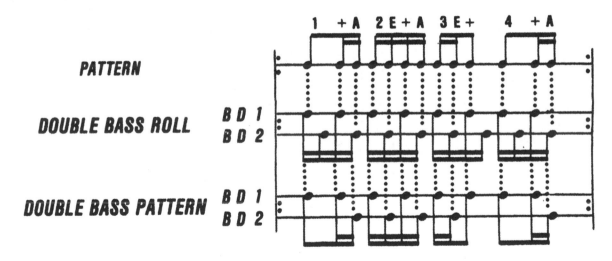

The following example illustrates how this system is used to break up an eighth note triplet pattern between two bass drums:

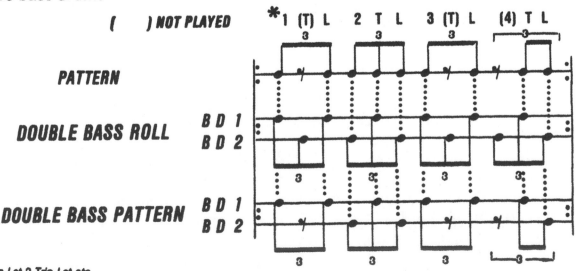

Here are a few rhythmic patterns that are broken up between two bass drums by using the Single Stroke System. The patterns on the left are in a sixteenth note feel and the patterns on the right are in an eighth note triplet feel. The first pattern in each column is the single stroke roll from which the patterns that follow are derived. Practice playing these patterns on the bass drums.

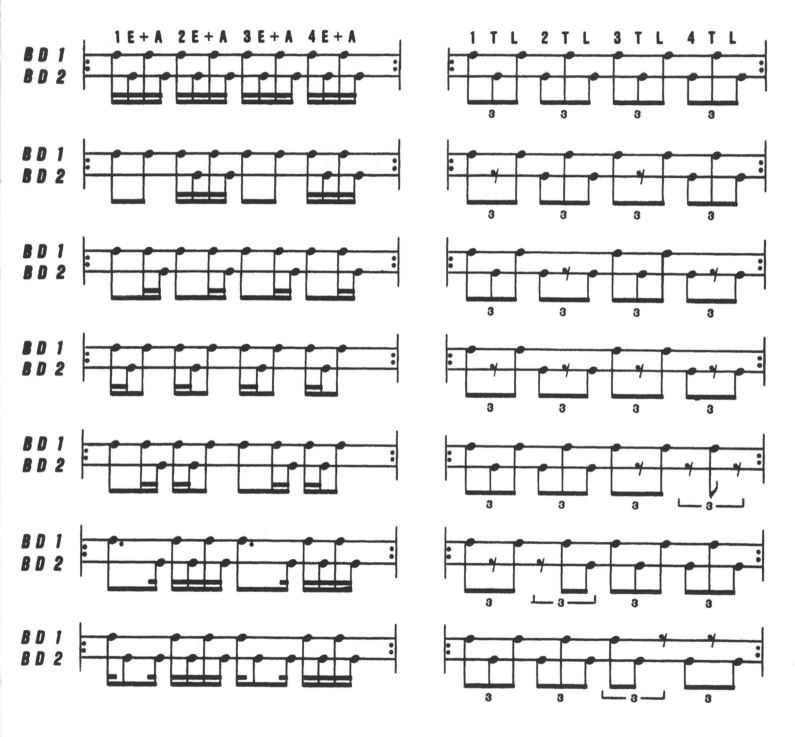

In Part I patterns similar to those above are used in playing BEATS. In Part II the Single Stroke System is applied to both hands and feet in playing FILLS. In Part III various hand patterns are played in SOLOING OVER THE DOUBLE BASS ROLL. All three parts deal with the sixteenth note feel (the "A" sections) and the eighth note triplet feel (the "B" sections). The introduction pages to each section will illustrate how this system is applied to that section. <u>Parts I, II and III should be studied simultaneously.</u>

There are instances when it is common to play B.D.2 (the bass drum on the hi hat side) on the downbeat of "1". A drummer who is used to playing eighth notes (on 1 + 2 + 3 + 4 +) with the hi hat foot can move the eighth notes over to B.D.2. By then playing the main bass drum, B.D.1, between the eighth notes (on E's and A's), the following sixteenth note roll is formed:

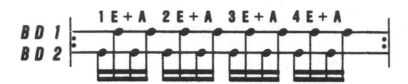

When playing the *continuous* sixteenth note roll, it will sound the same regardless of which foot is used to lead. However, when playing *non-continuous* or *"broken"* rhythmic patterns or when coming out of fills that combine hands and feet, it is desirable to play the main bass drum on the downbeat of "1".

Another example of when it is common to play B.D.2 on the downbeat of "1" is the eighth note triplet shuffle:

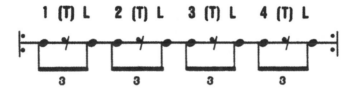

A drummer who is used to playing quarter notes (on 1, 2, 3, 4) with the hi hat foot can play the shuffle as:

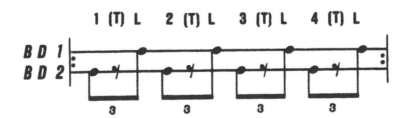

This method of playing the shuffle is especially effective at fast tempos. Alternate ways of playing the shuffle and other 2-note triplet patterns are discussed on page 30.

PART I   DOUBLE BASS BEATS

In Part I rhythmic patterns are broken up systematically between the two bass drums. They are played together with a RIDE and SNARE to form beats. Part IA deals with sixteenth note patterns and Part IB with eighth note triplet patterns.

A suggested way to practice each beat is to first play the double bass pattern, then add the RIDE and SNARE. Another approach is to first play the RIDE and SNARE with B.D 1, then add B.D.2.

After playing Part I as written, try using the alternate RIDE patterns that are suggested before each section Experiment with some of your own RIDE and SNARE patterns.

PART IA   SIXTEENTH NOTE PATTERNS

In this section patterns using sixteenth notes are broken up between the two bass drums. They are played together with an eighth note RIDE and the SNARE on "2" and "4" to form beats. The following beat illustrates the sixteenth note double bass roll:

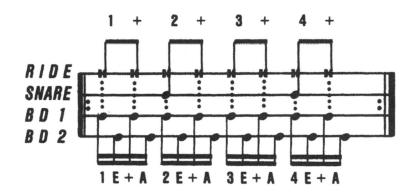

When playing the sixteenth note double bass roll together with an eighth note RIDE, B.D.1 and the RIDE both play the same eighth note pattern. By playing B D.2 between the notes of B D 1 (all the E's and A's), the sixteenth note roll is formed

Practice playing the above beat. The more familiar you are with playing the *continuous* roll, the easier it will be to play the *broken* patterns in this section.

Using the Single Stroke System, sixteenth note patterns are broken up between the two bass drums as follows:

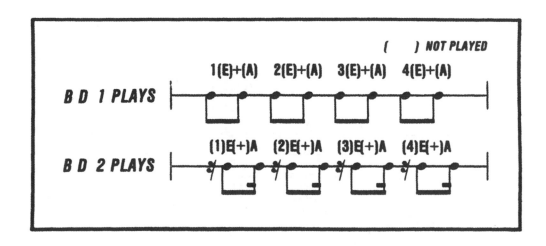

Here are the different 1-beat patterns that can be formed by breaking up the sixteenth note grouping (1E+A). The figure beneath each pattern shows how it is played on the two bass drums.

SIXTEENTH NOTE PATTERNS

Here are some examples of beats using sixteenth note bass drum patterns.

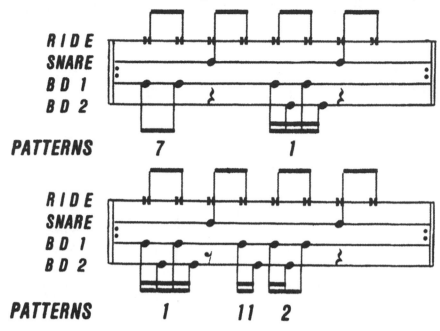

The beats in this section are written with an eighth note RIDE Here are some suggestions for other RIDE patterns.

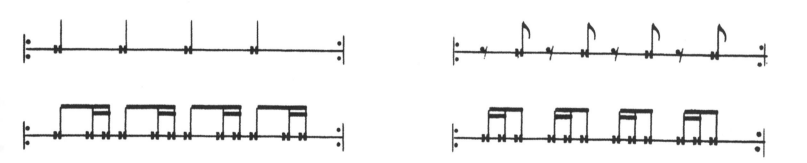

Since most of the bass drum patterns in this section are designed around a "2" and "4" backbeat on the snare, any hand pattern with accents on "2" and "4" can be used. Try some patterns from PART III A2 For example, the single paradiddle (RLRR LRLL RLRR LRLL), with R playing the RIDE and L playing the SNARE.

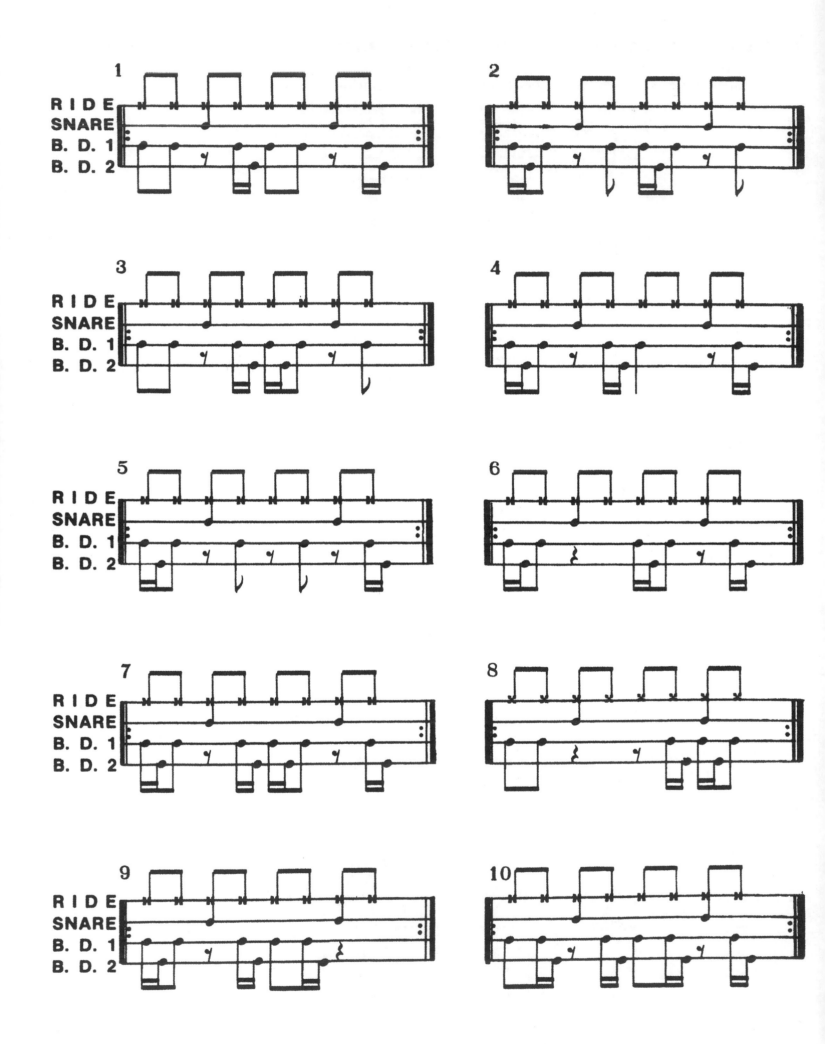

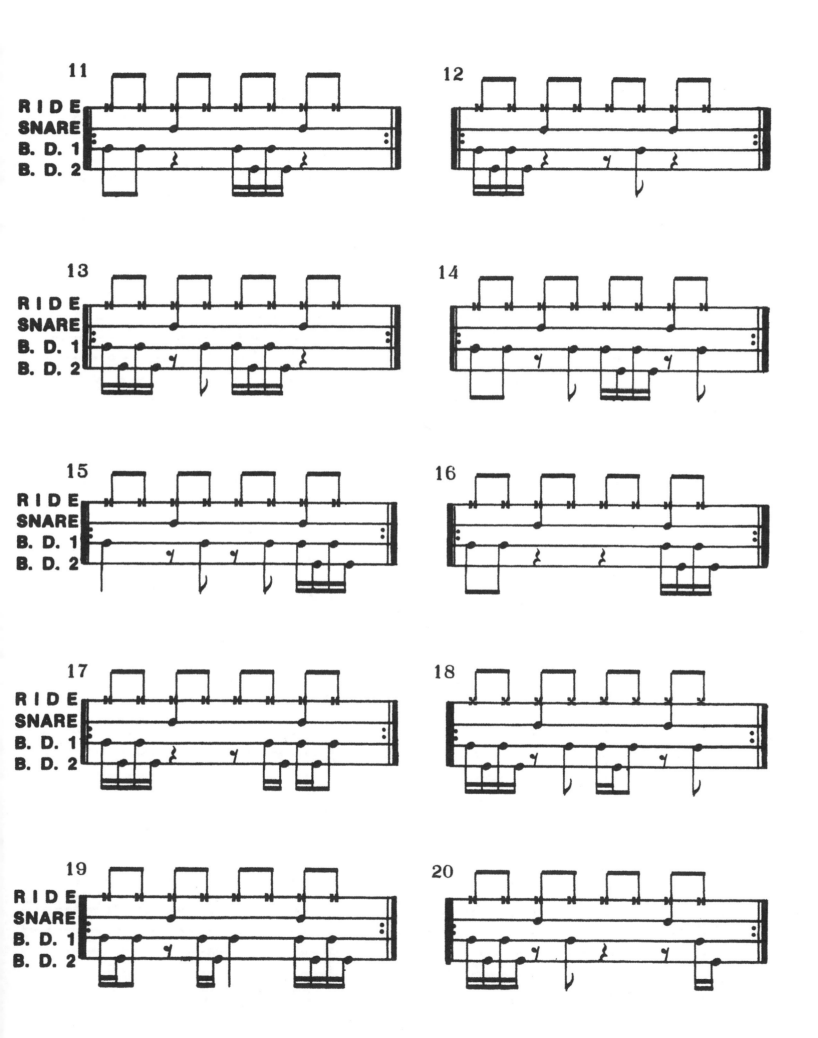

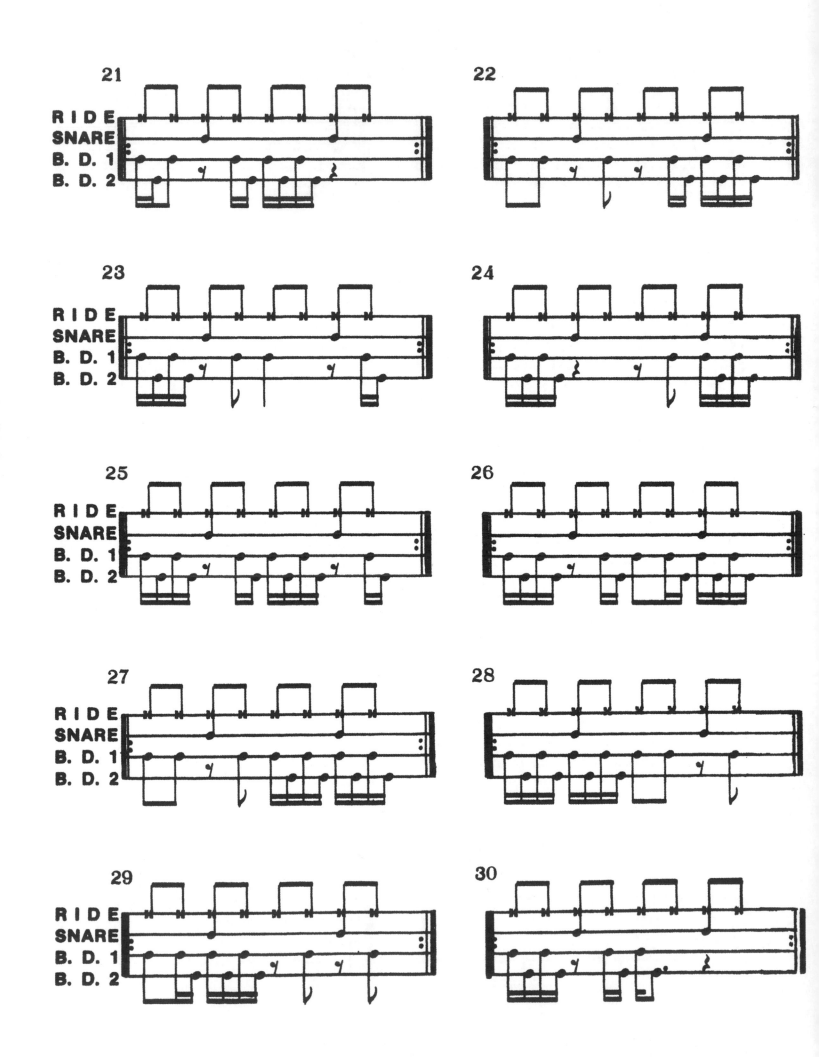

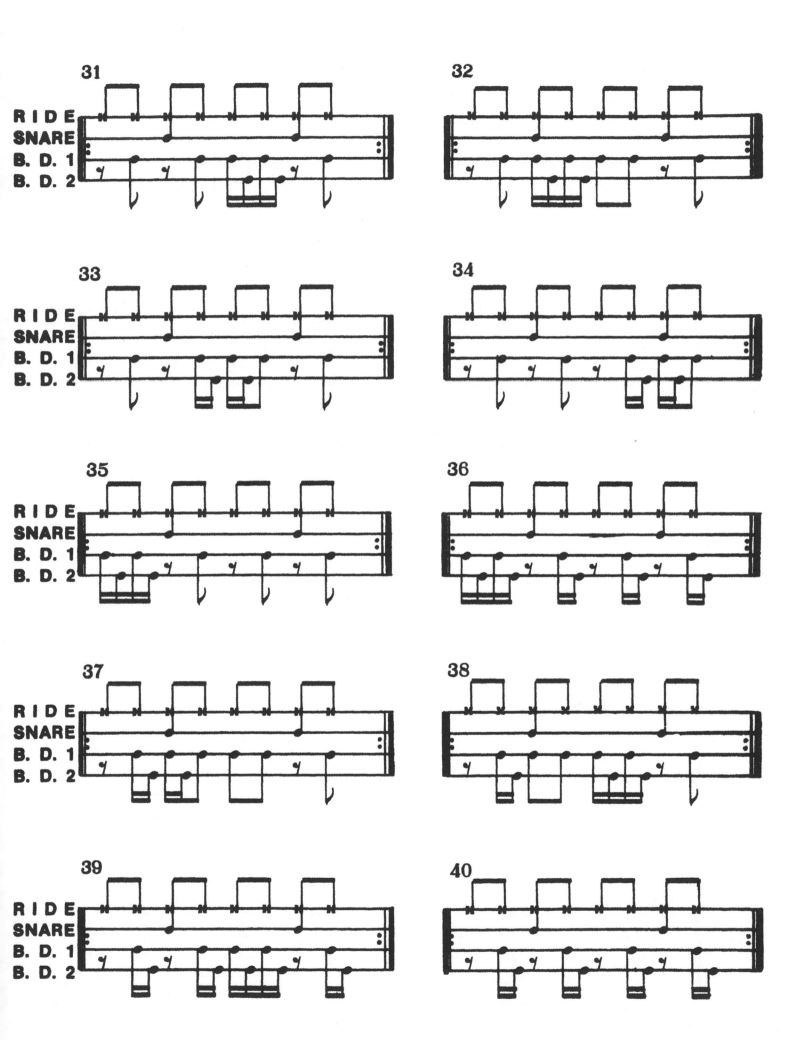

13

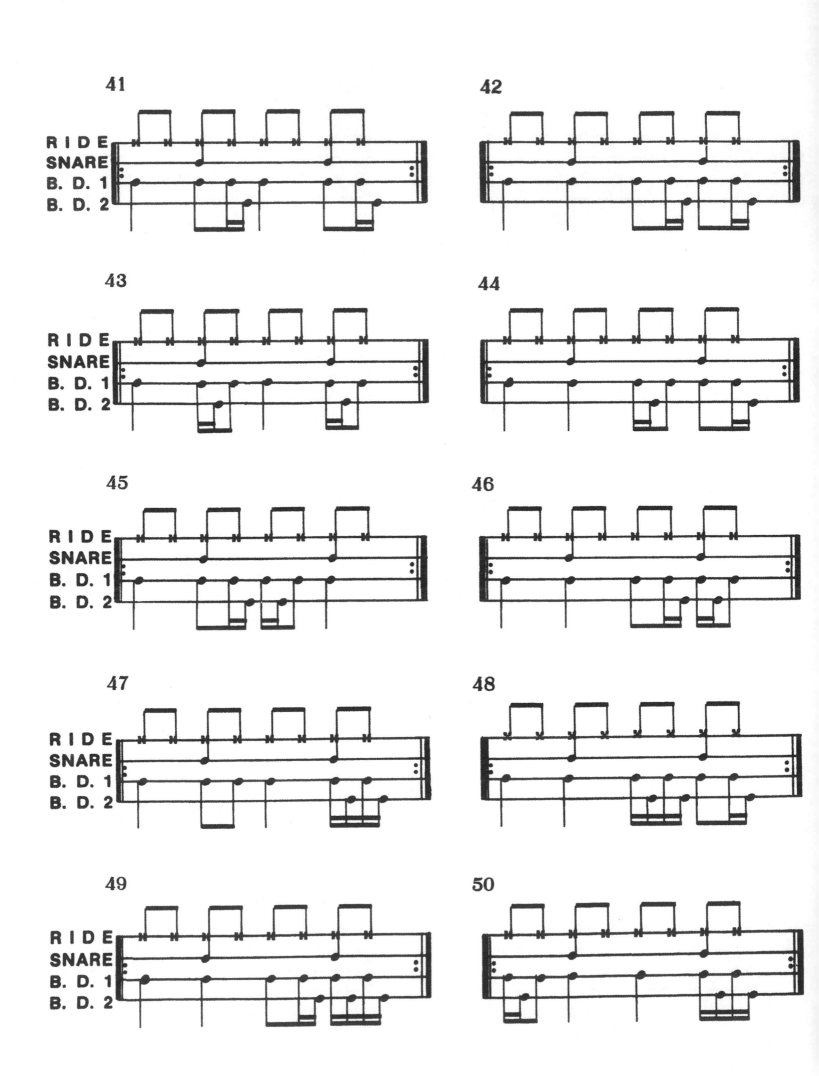

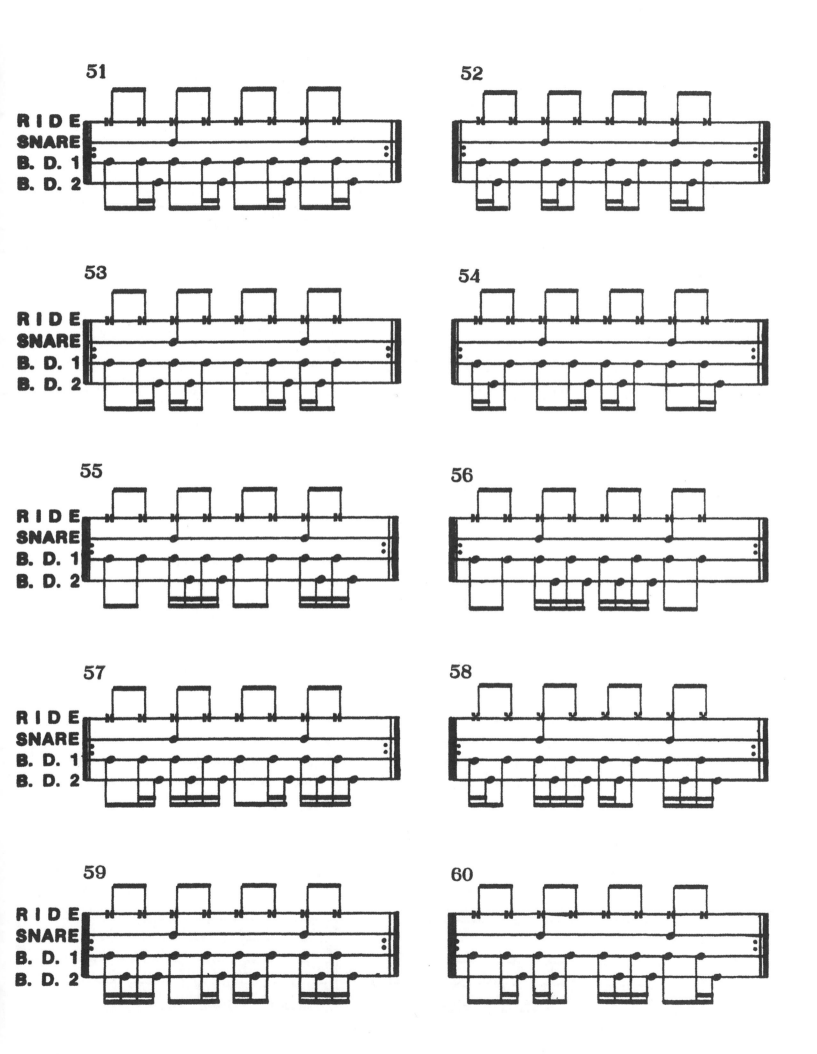

15

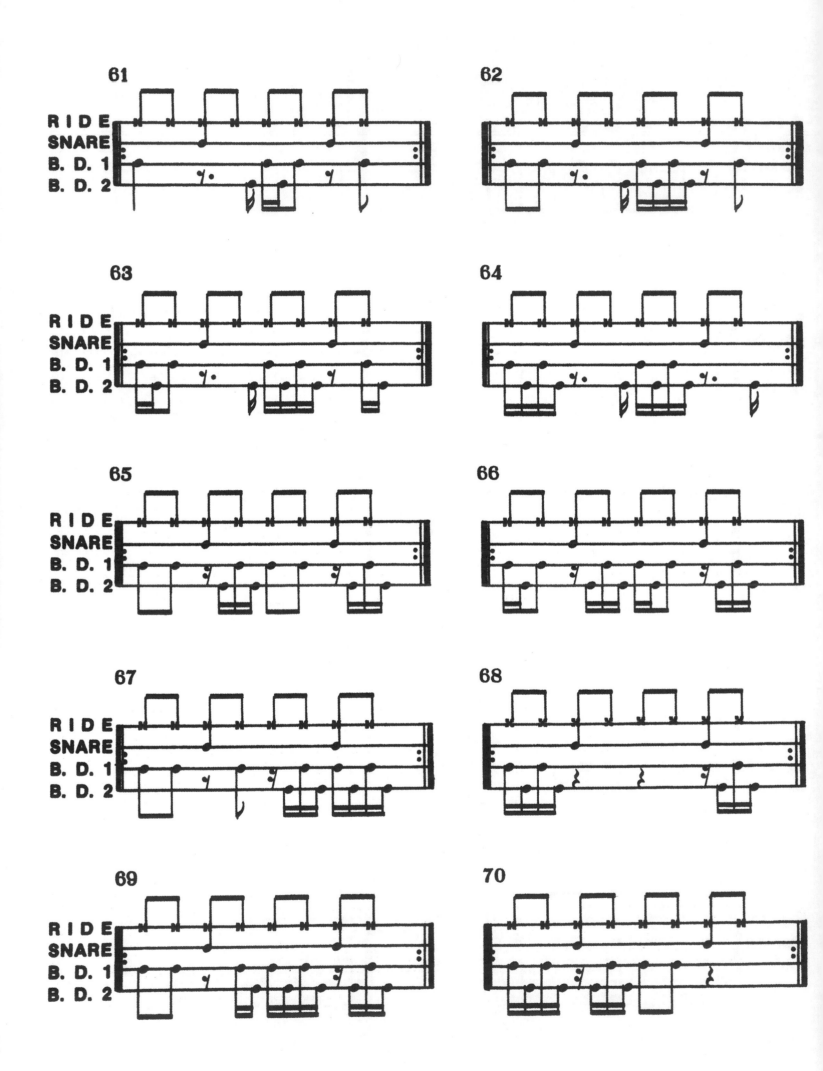

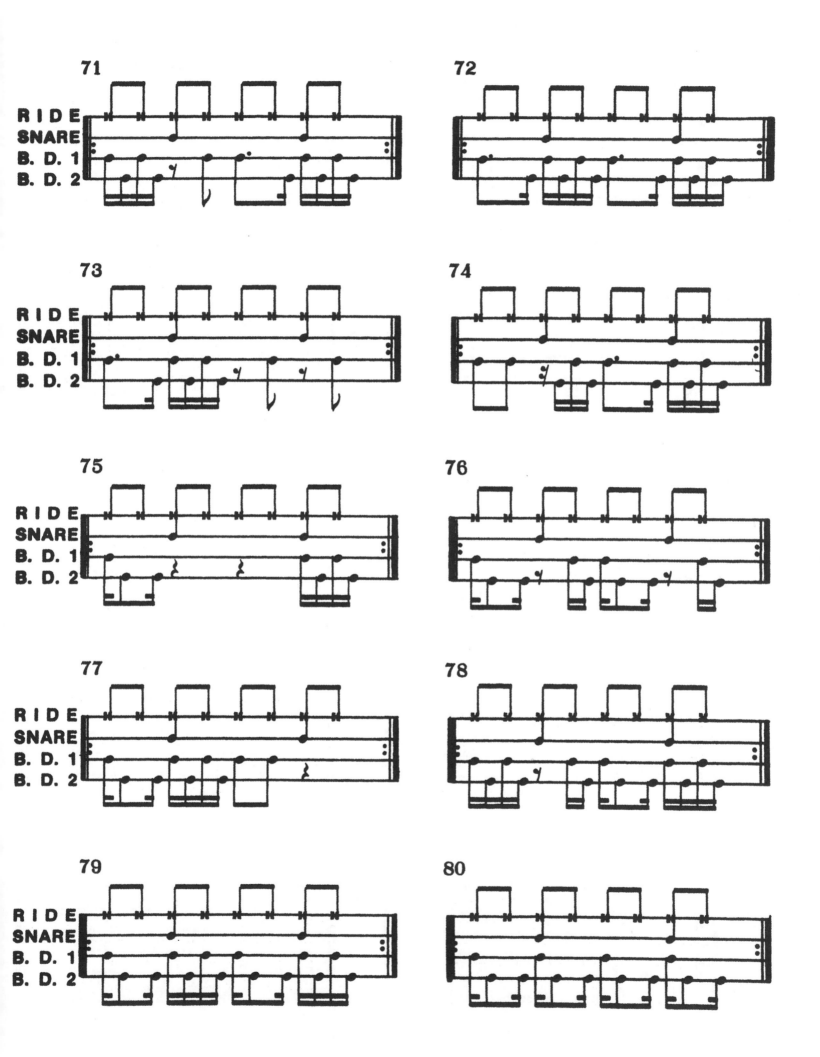

17

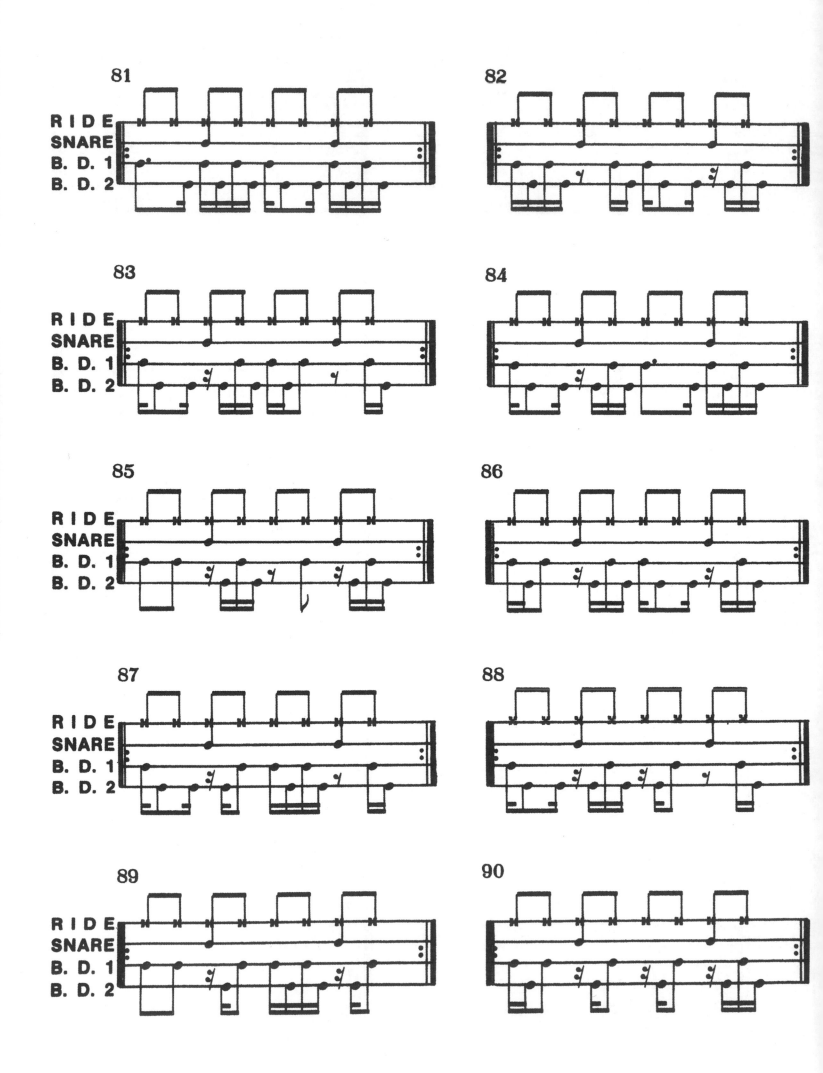

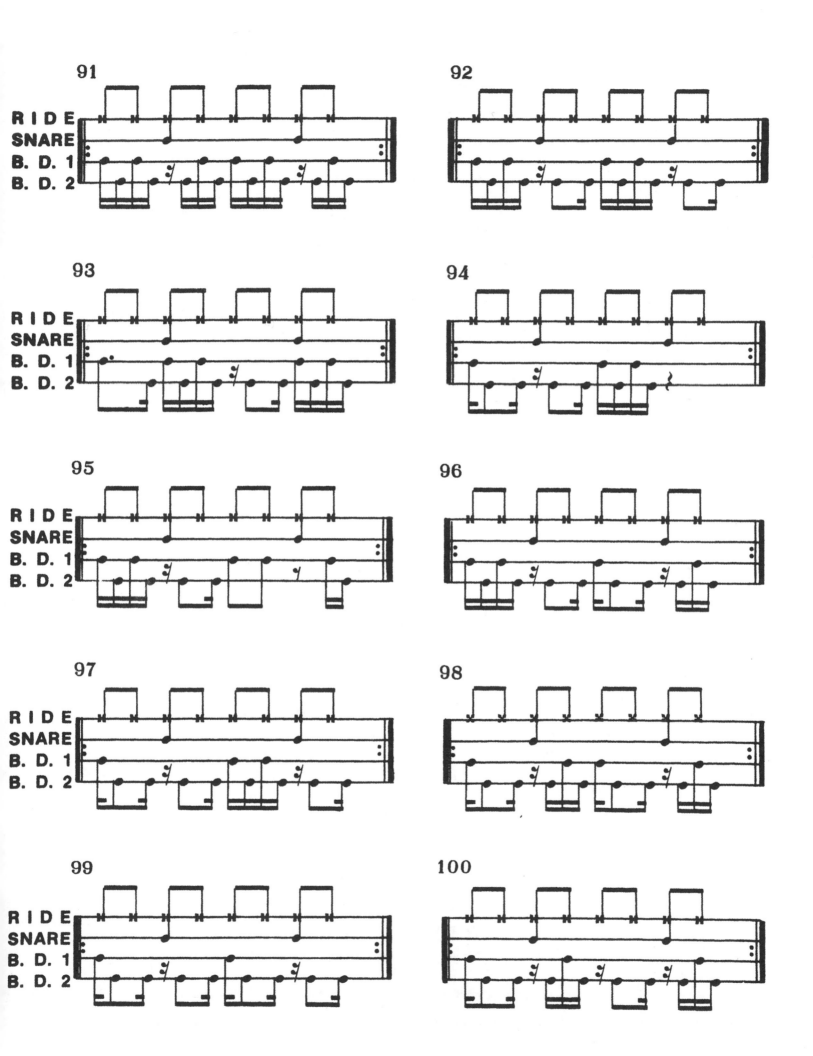

PART IB   EIGHTH NOTE TRIPLET PATTERNS

In this section patterns using eighth note triplets are broken up between the two bass drums. They are played together with a quarter note RIDE and the SNARE on "2" and "4" to form beats. The following beat illustrates the eighth note triplet double bass roll:

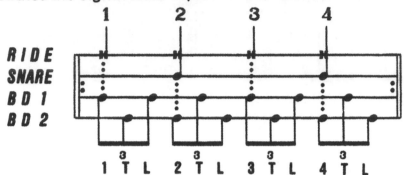

When playing the eighth note triplet double bass roll, B.D.1 plays two quarter note triplets per measure of 4/4:

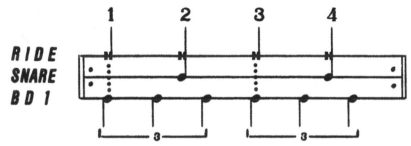

which can be broken down to:

In the following beat B.D.1 is played together with the RIDE and SNARE:

When played together over a complete measure of 4/4, B.D 1 plays 6 notes while the RIDE plays 4. This is known as a 6:4 (6 against 4) polyrhythm. The RIDE and B.D 1 both fall together on "1" and "3". *Keep in mind that the two quarter note triplets on B.D.1 are 6 notes of equal duration. They are evenly spaced throughout the measure.* By playing B.D.2 between the notes of B.D.1, the eighth note triplet roll is formed. The RIDE, SNARE and B.D.2 all fall together on "2" and "4"

Practice playing both of the above beats. Again, the more familiar you are with playing the *continuous* roll, the easier it will be to play the *broken* patterns in this section.

Using the Single Stroke System, eighth note triplet patterns are broken up between the two bass drums as follows:

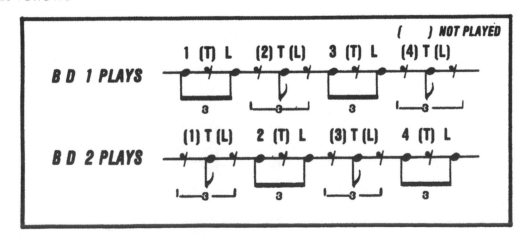

The eighth note triplet roll differs from the sixteenth note roll in that the main bass drum (B D 1) will fall on every other beat ("1" and "3"). Therefore, a 1-beat eighth note triplet pattern will be played one way (A) if it falls on "1" or "3", and the opposite way (B) if it falls on "2" or "4" Both (A) and (B) are illustrated in the triplet patterns that follow:

Eighth Note Triplet Patterns

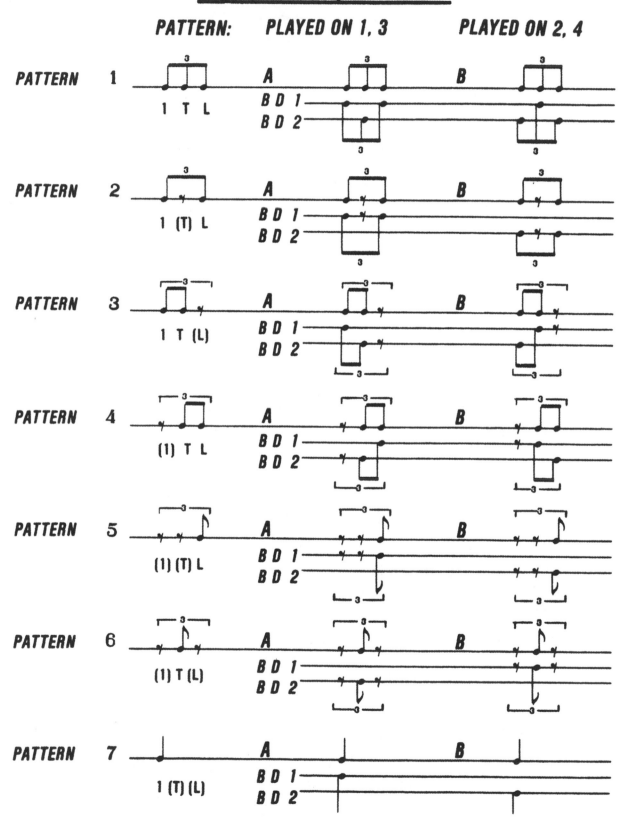

Here are some examples of beats using eighth note triplet bass drum patterns:

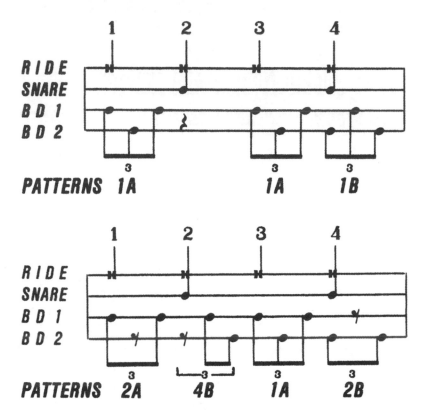

PATTERNS 1A   1A   1B

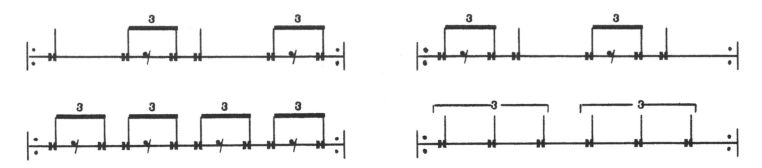

PATTERNS 2A   4B   1A   2B

The beats in this section are written with a quarter note RIDE Here are some suggestions for other RIDE patterns:

As with the sixteenth note beats, most of the bass drum patterns in this section are designed around a "2" and "4" snare pattern Any triplet hand pattern with a snare accent on the "2" and "4" can be played with these bass drum patterns. For example, the single stroke roll (RLR-LRL-RLR-LRL) with R playing the RIDE and L playing the SNARE.

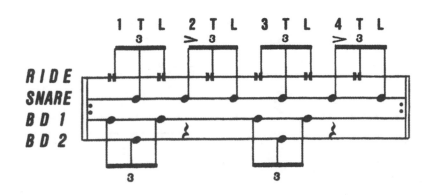

22

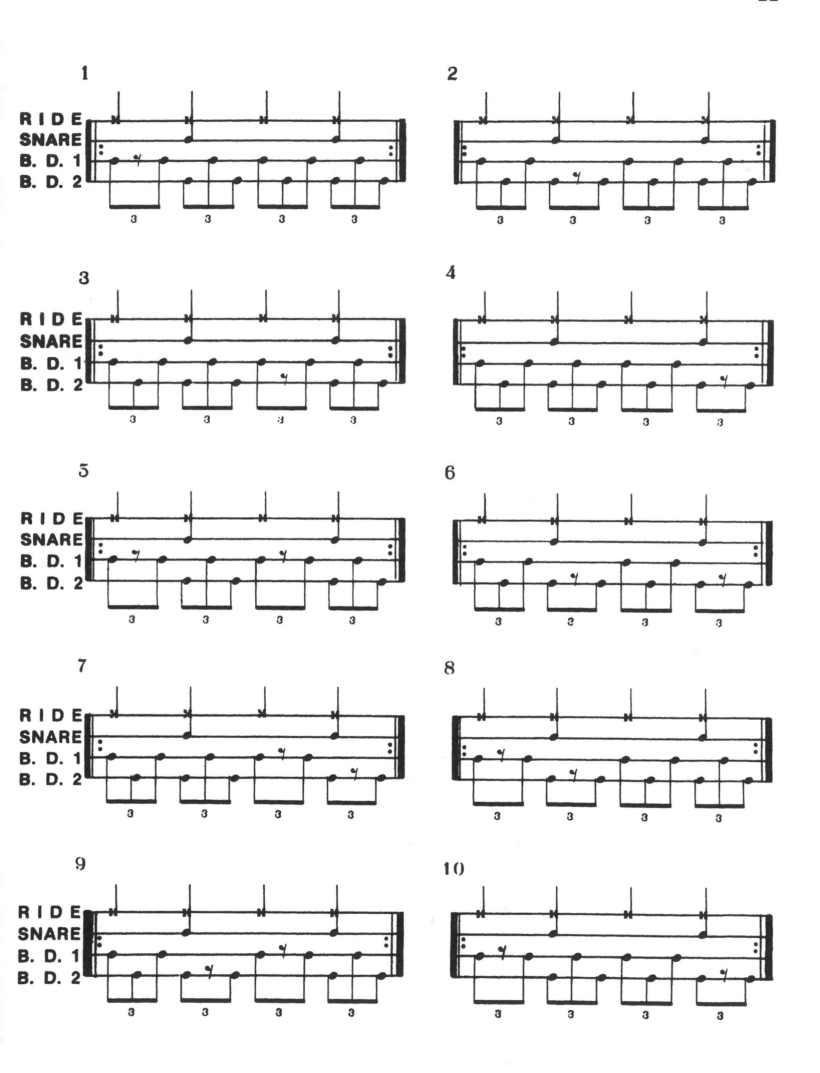

23

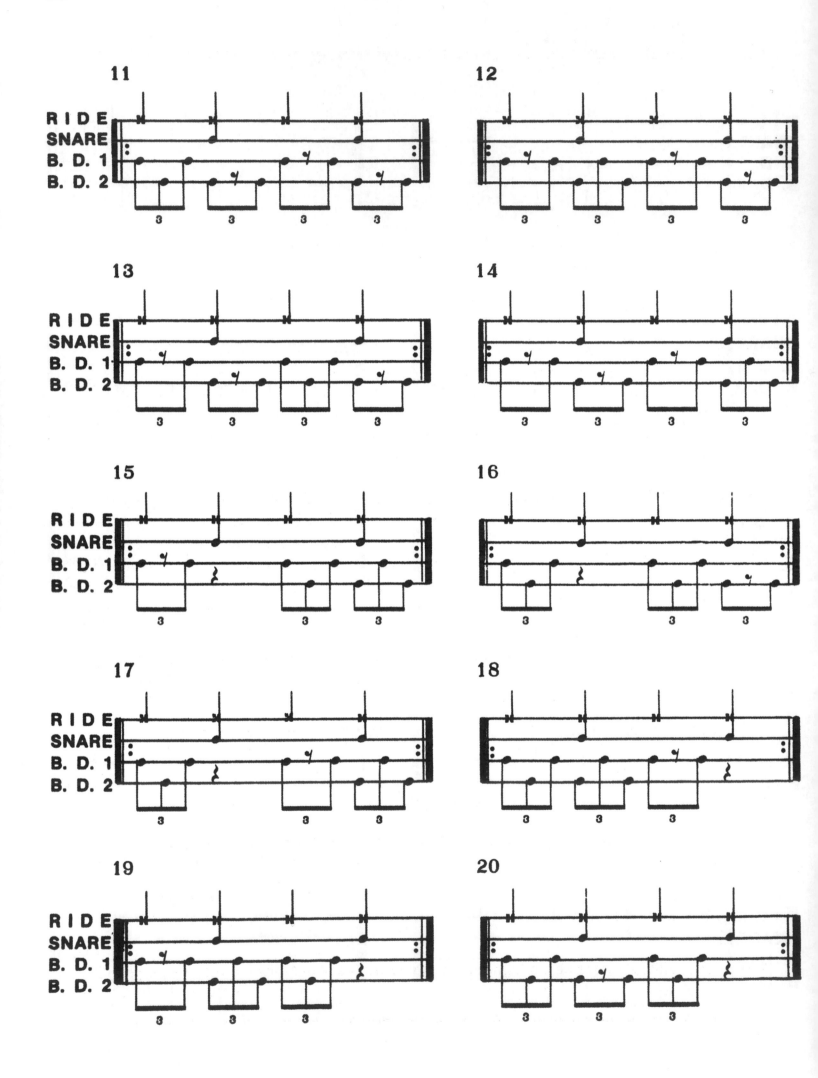

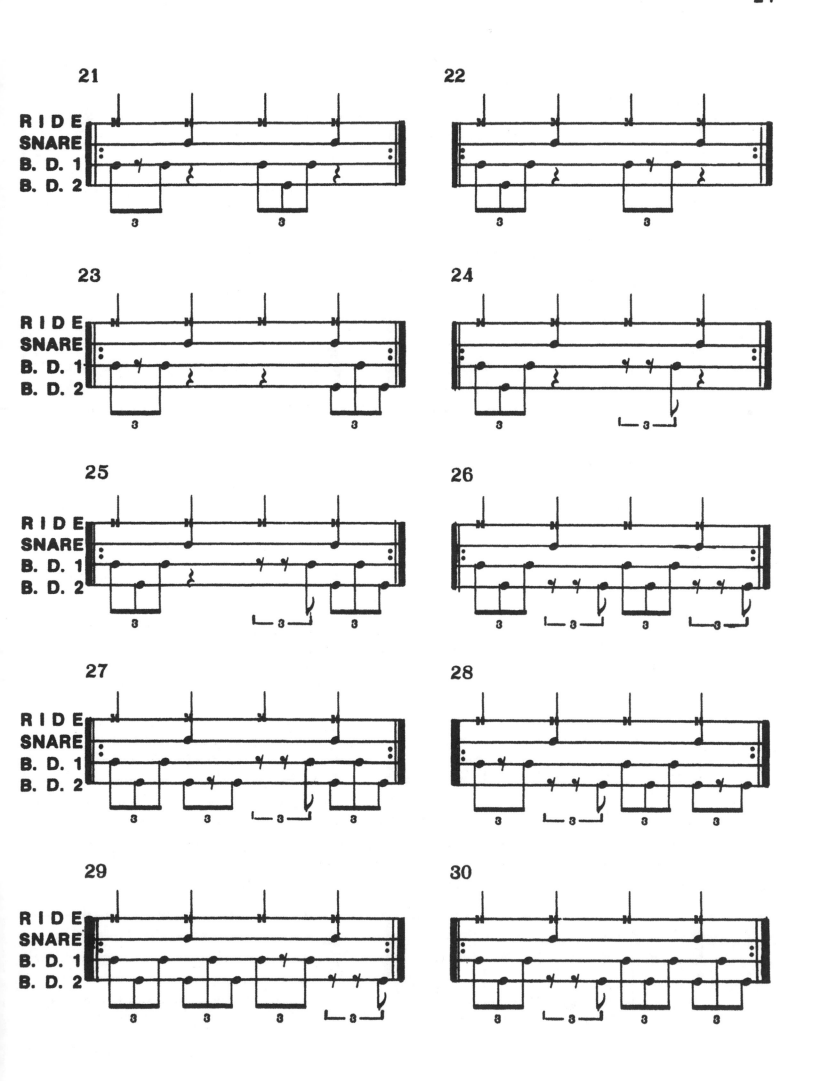

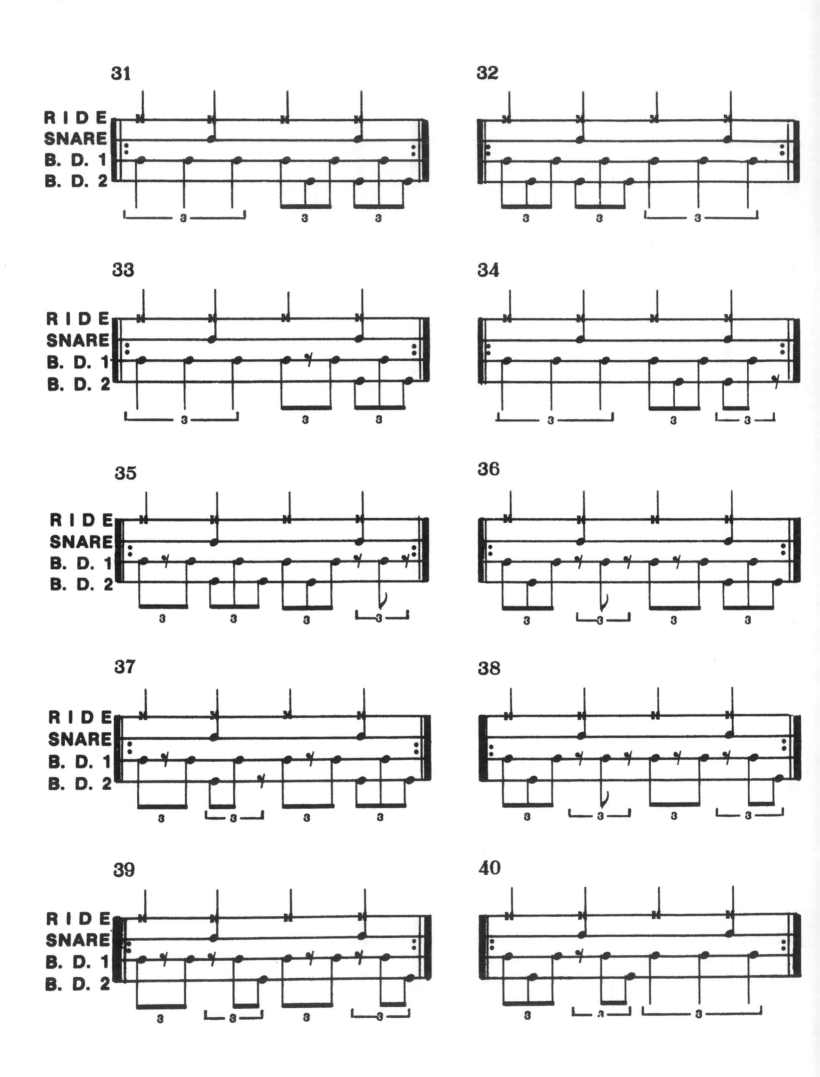

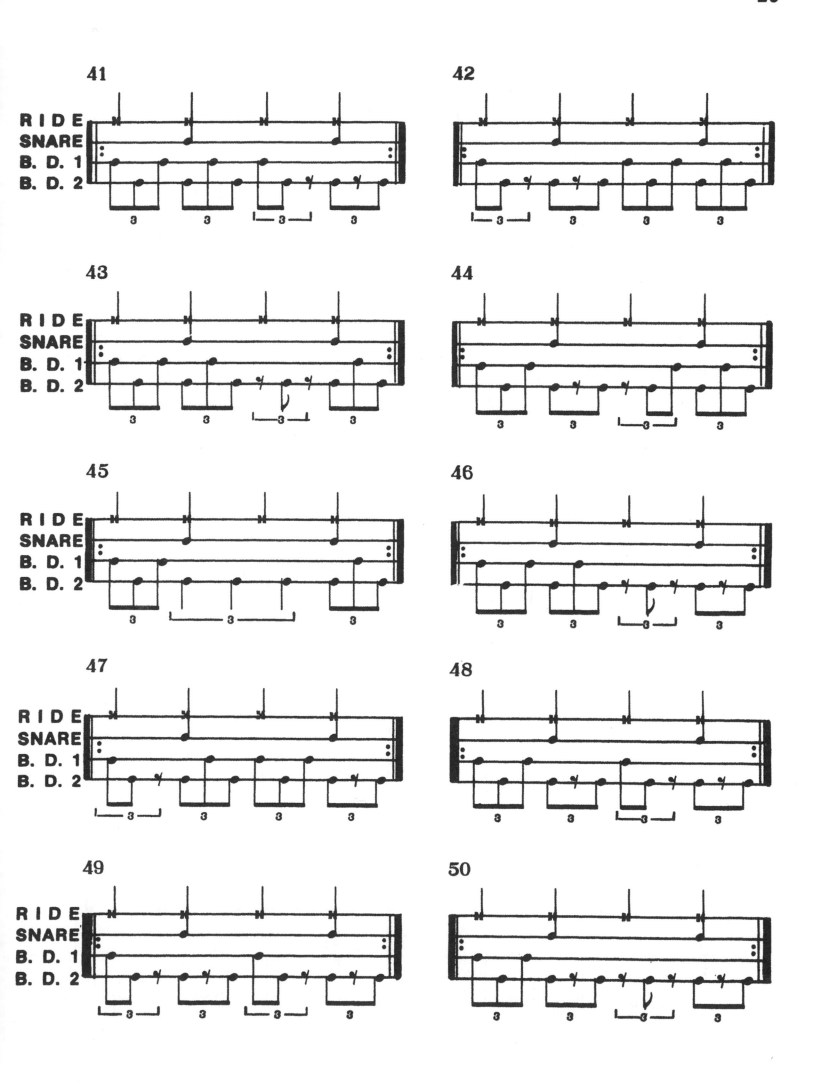

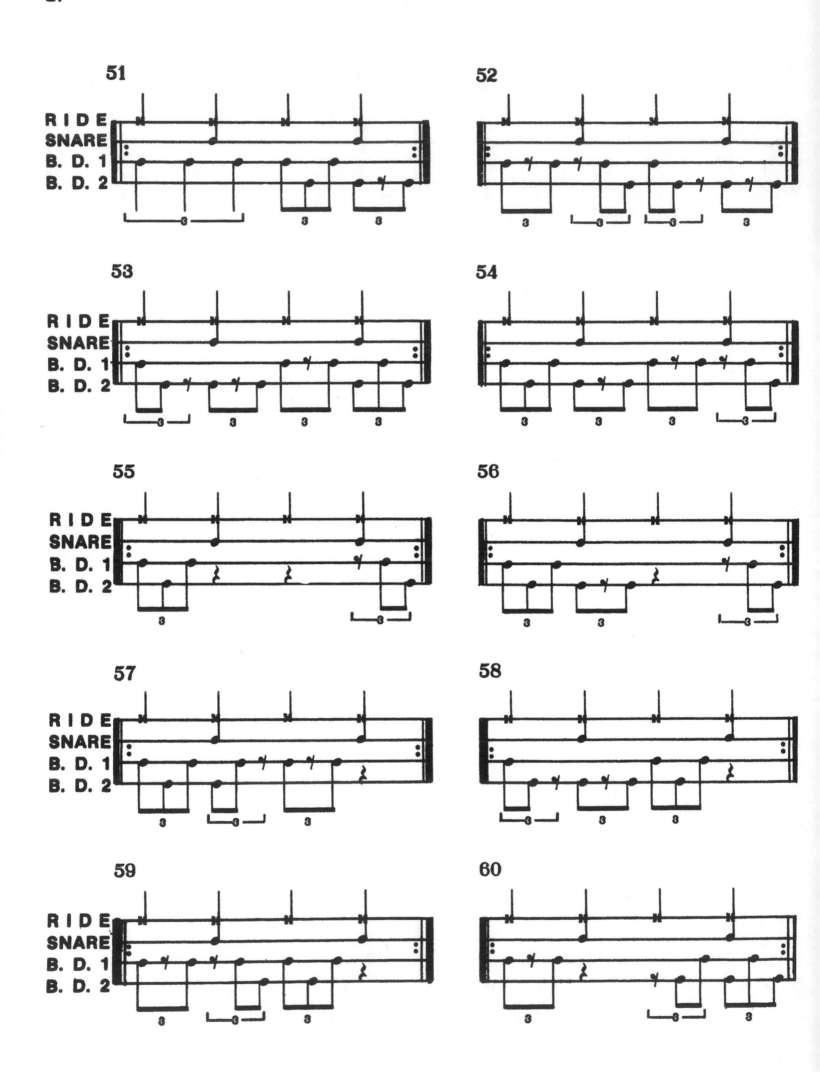

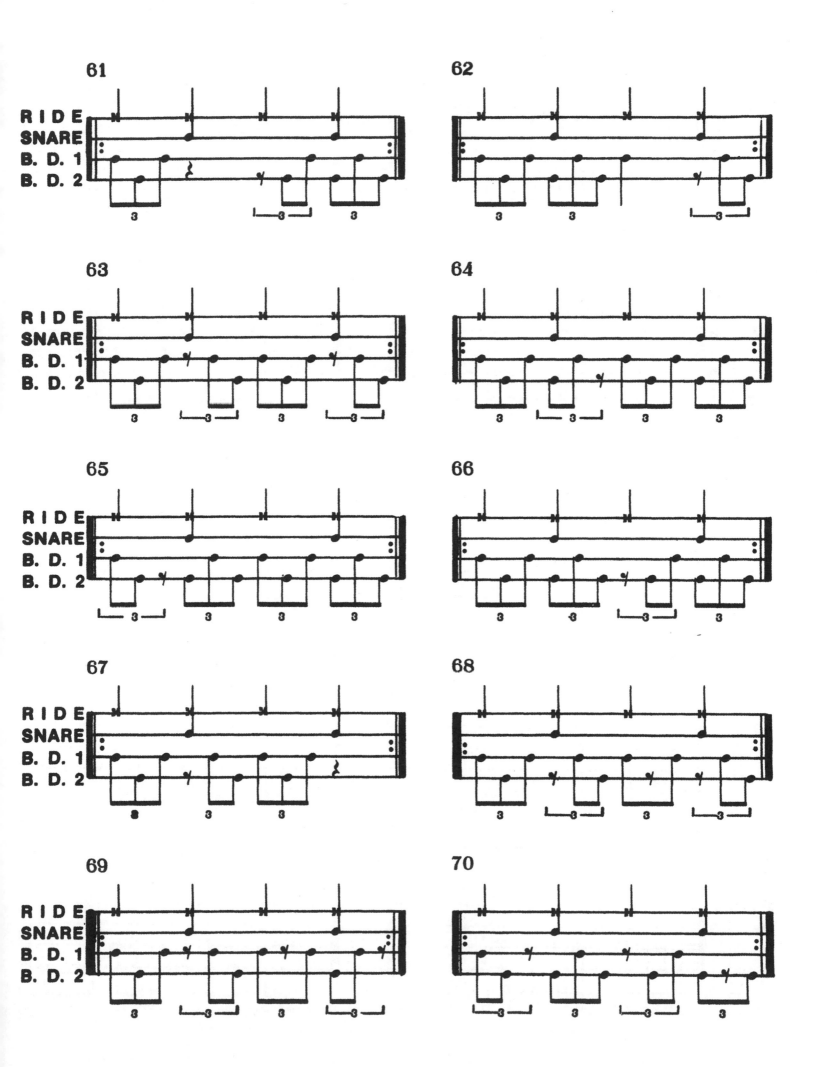

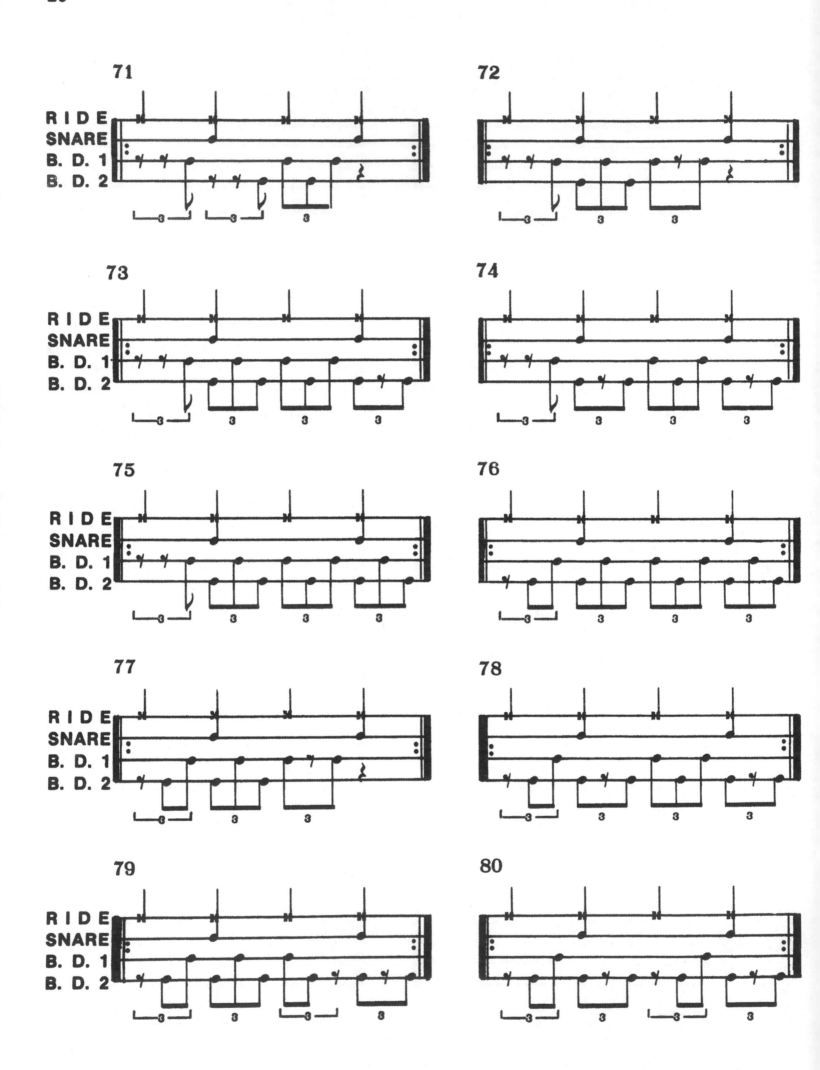

Two-Note Triplet Patterns

There is a unique situation that occurs when playing one of the following 2-note triplet patterns repeatedly on two bass drums.

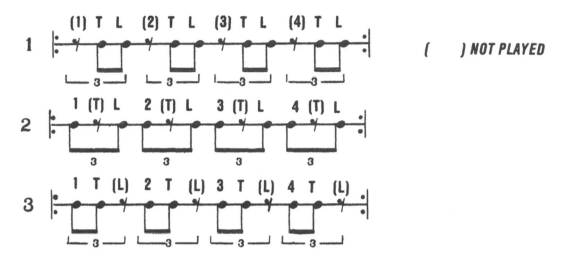

( ) NOT PLAYED

Since the same two notes are played in every beat of the measure, you may want to play the bass drums in a constant sequence (B D 1, 2-1, 2-1, 2-etc or B D 2, 1-2, 1-2, 1-etc) rather than alternating the sequence on every beat of the measure (B D 1, 2-2, 1-1, 2-2, 1-etc)

The bass drum patterns in the following beats are written three ways (A, B, C) The first two (A and B) use a constant sequence for B D 1 and B D.2 The third (C) uses the Single Stroke System which will alternate the sequence of B D 1 and B D.2 on every beat of the measure. Try each variation, in a playing situation use the variation that sounds best.

* *NOTE: The SNARE is played on the last note of each triplet. This beat will flow better this way.*

PART II

DOUBLE BASS FILLS

In Part II patterns are broken up systematically between both hands and both feet These patterns can be used as 1-bar fills. They can also be repeated or combined with each other to form extended fills and solos. Part IIA deals with sixteenth notes and Part IIB with eighth note triplets. The top line of each pattern will be labeled "HANDS" and can be played on different drums. For example, in the following pattern the HANDS are played on the SNARE.

The HANDS can also be broken up between the SNARE and TOM. For example, the same pattern can be played as.

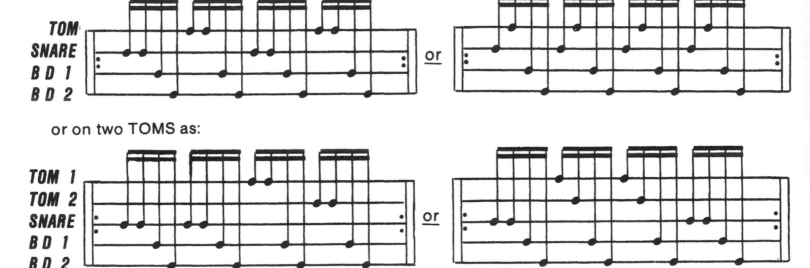

or on two TOMS as:

Try playing these patterns in other ways depending on the different drums in your kit

Every fill pattern in Part II is paired with its' "mirror-image" in which the feet play the part of the hands and vice-versa. For example, the above pattern will be paired as follows.

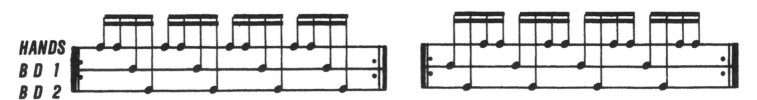

Practice playing these fills together with a beat similar to those suggested in each section For example, play phrases such as.

    3 bar beat — 1 bar fill
    1 bar beat — 1 bar fill
    2 bar beat — 2 bar fill (play a 1-bar fill two times or combine two different
                            1-bar fills).

Once you are familiar with these patterns, try combining them as extended fills or solos of 4, 8, 16 or more measures.

PART IIA   SIXTEENTH NOTE FILLS

In this section fills are formed by breaking up continuous sixteenth notes between both hands and both feet. When playing these fills, use the Single Stroke System for both your hands and feet. That is, start with your lead hand or foot and then alternate strokes. In the following illustration, HAND 1 refers to the lead hand, and HAND 2 to the other. Here is the key to playing these fills:

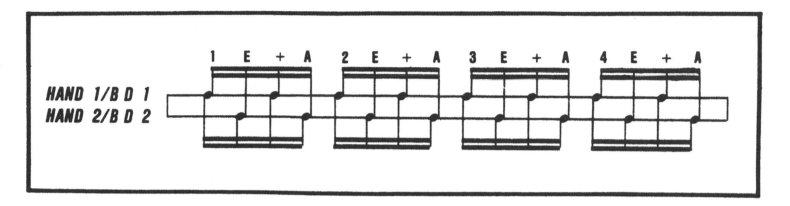

By using this system your lead hand and foot will fall on the "1" of the measure following the fill. For example, for a right-handed player·

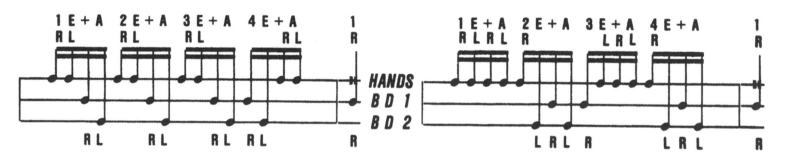

In both cases, the righty will be on the right hand and foot after the fill.

Although every fill in Part II is 1-bar long and starts on the downbeat of "1", this system can be used regardless of the length of a fill or where it starts. The following examples illustrate fills that start in different places of the measure:

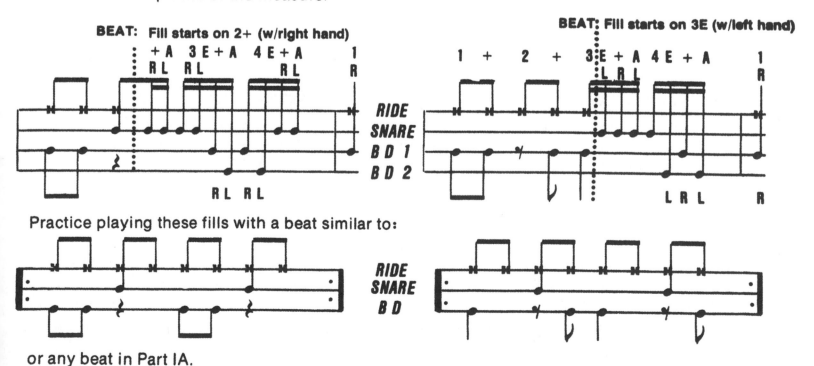

Practice playing these fills with a beat similar to:

or any beat in Part IA.

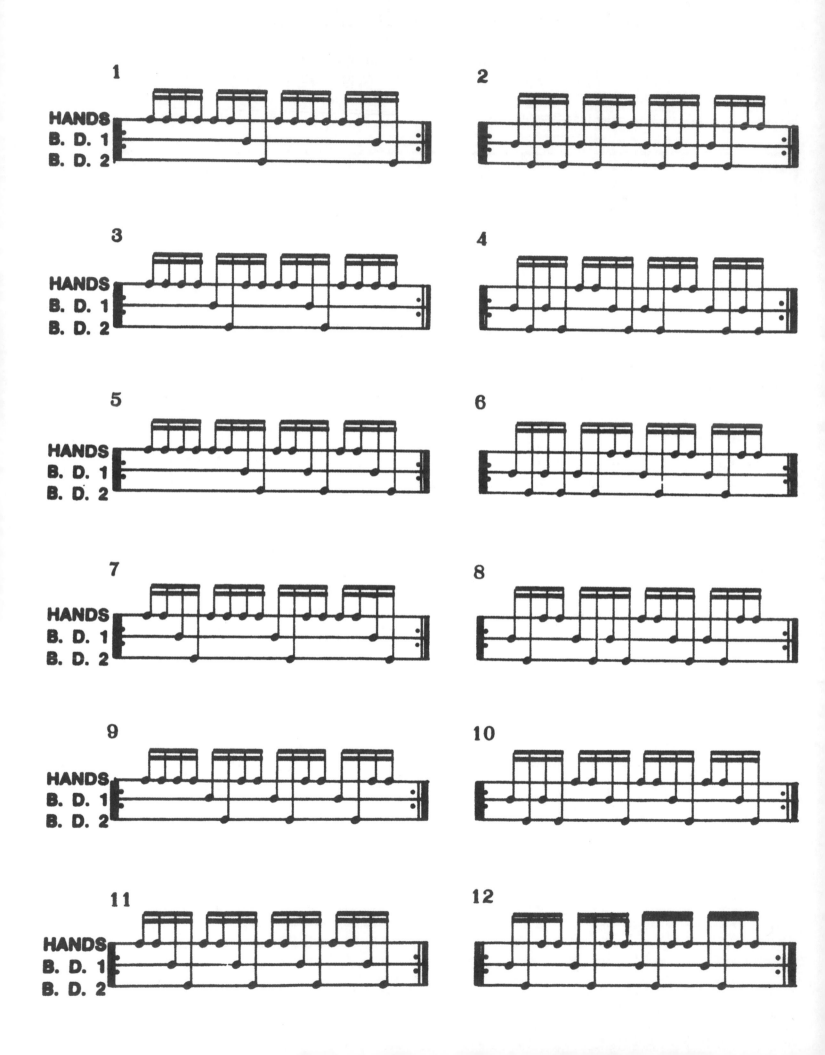

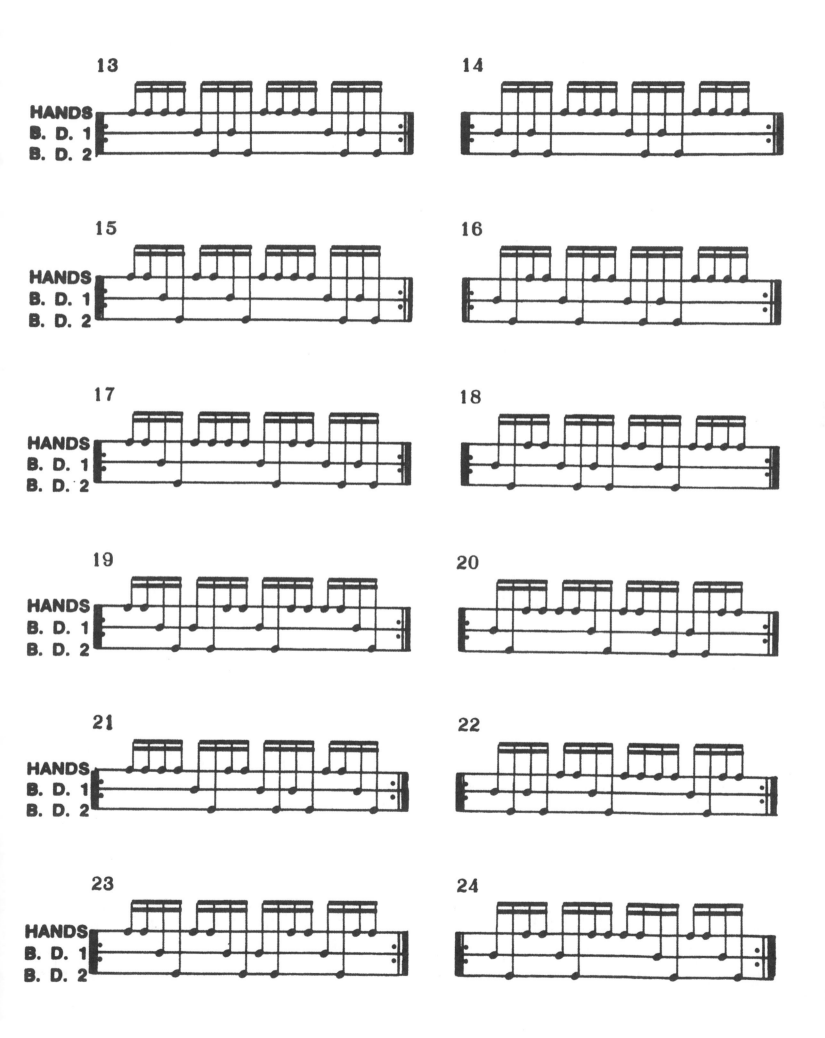

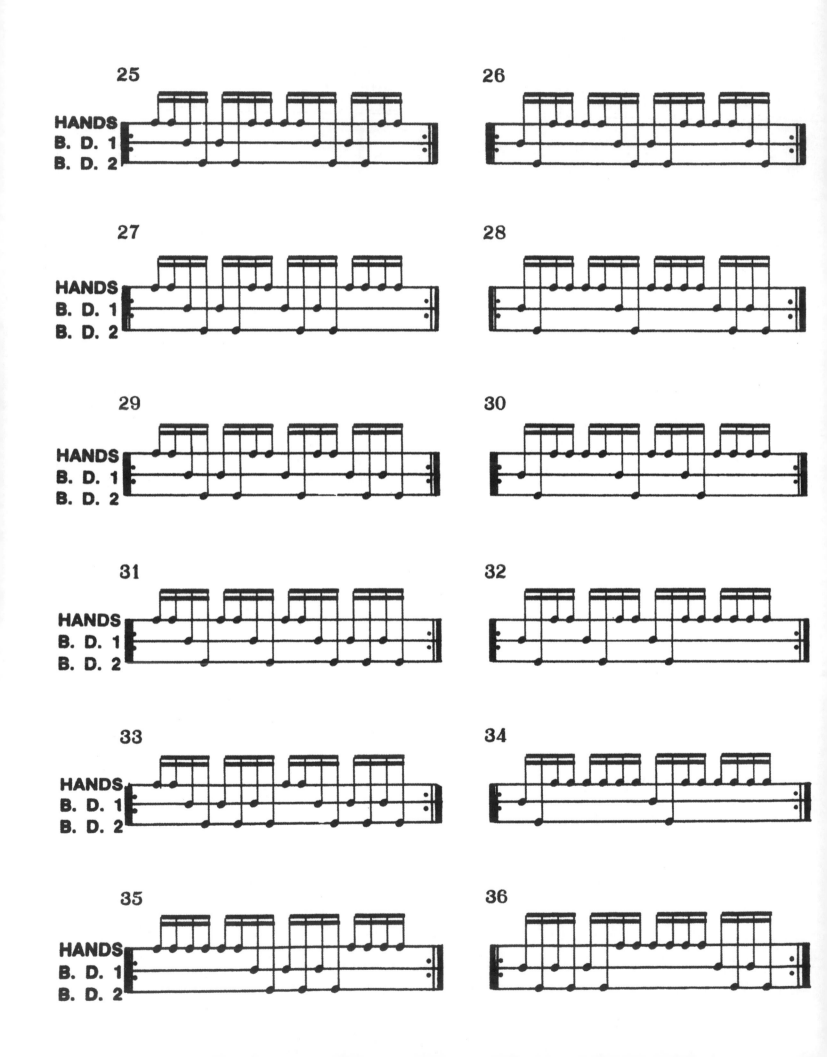

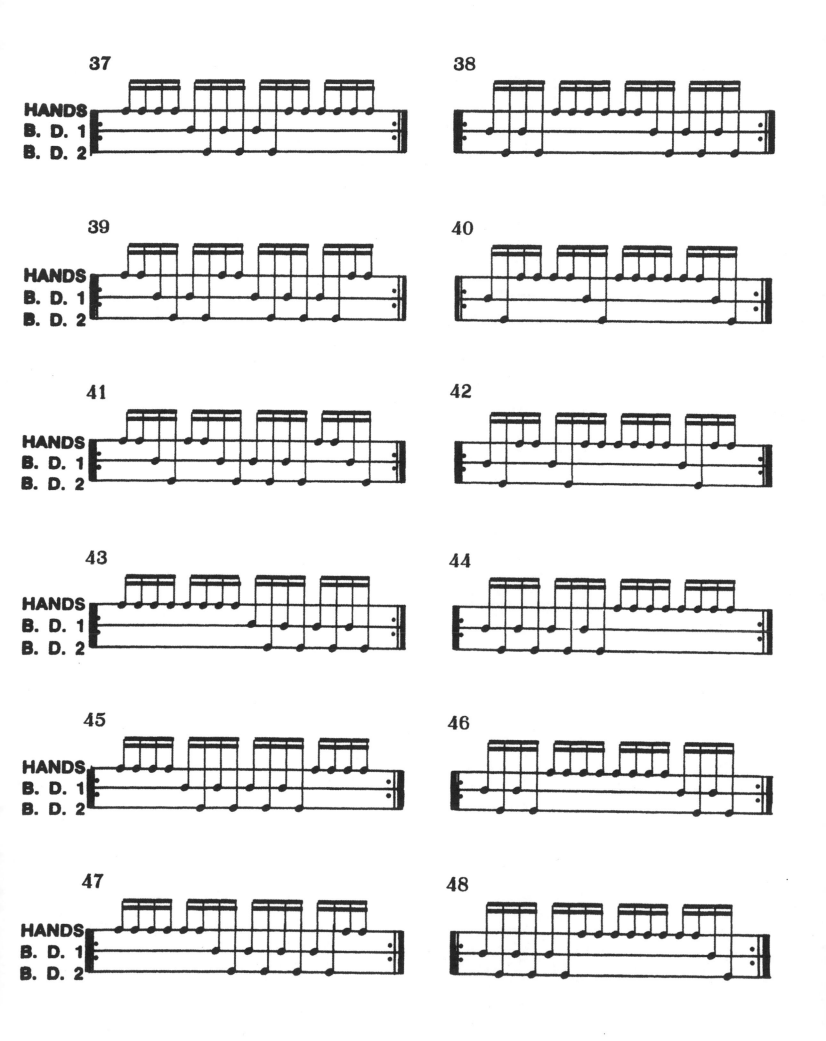

37

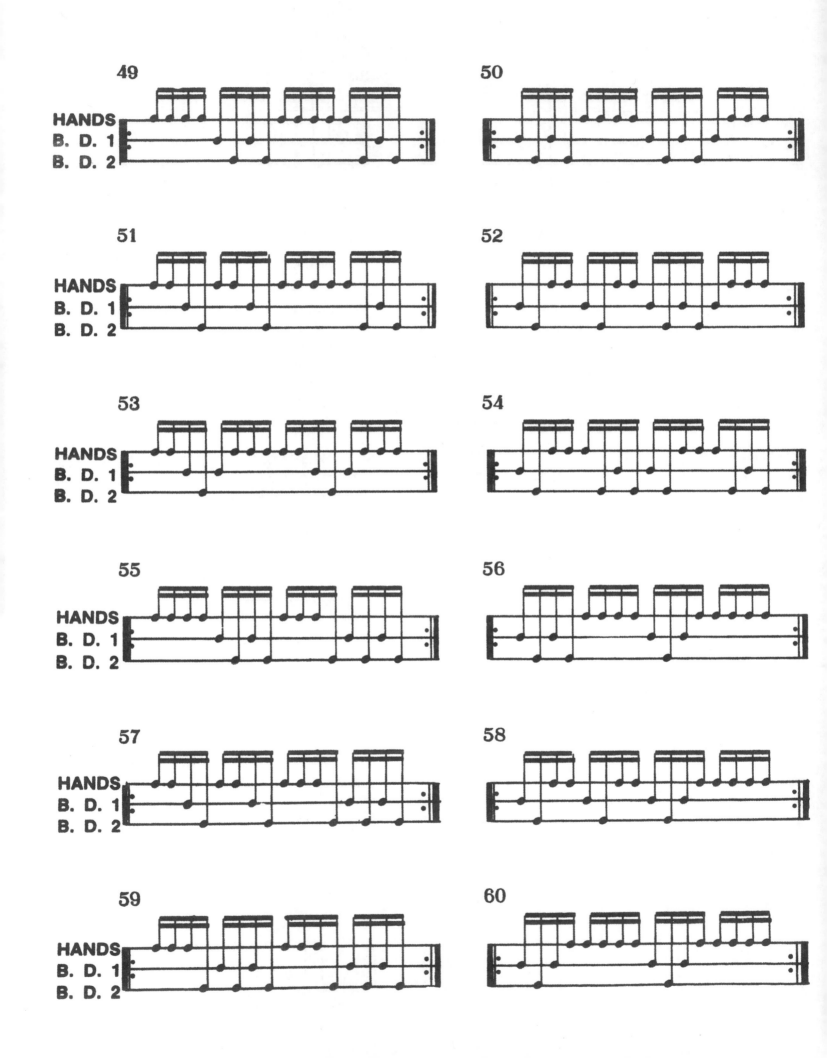

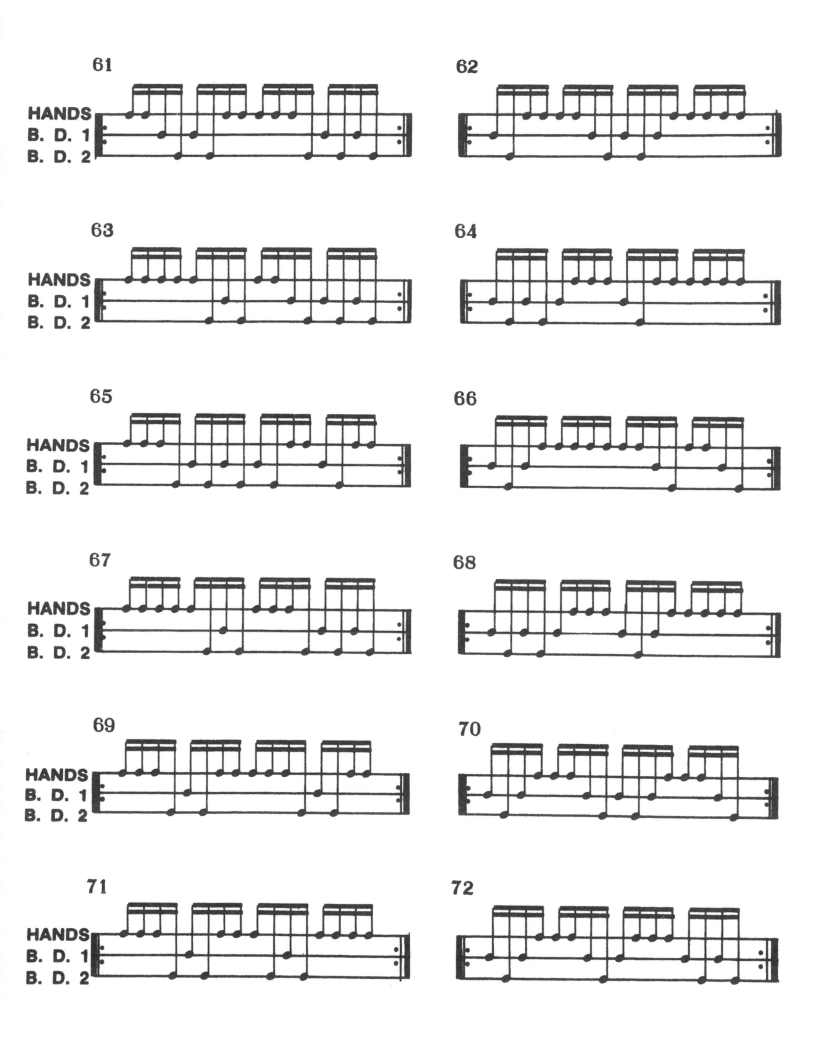

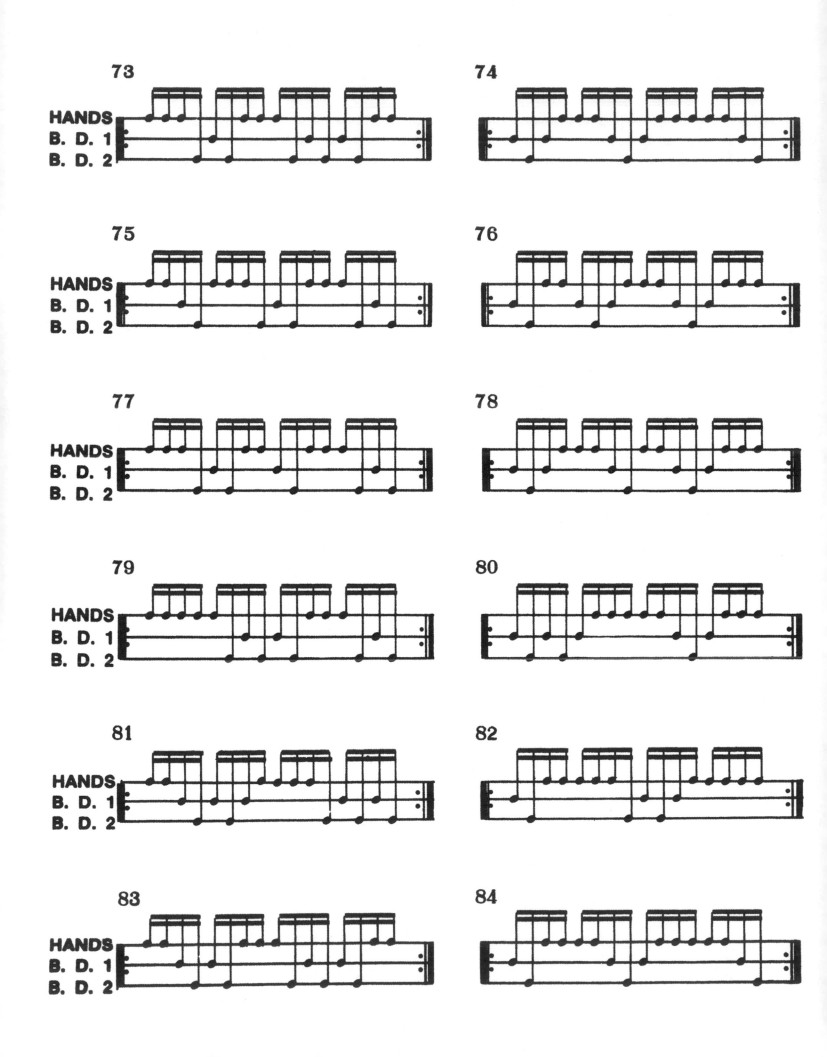

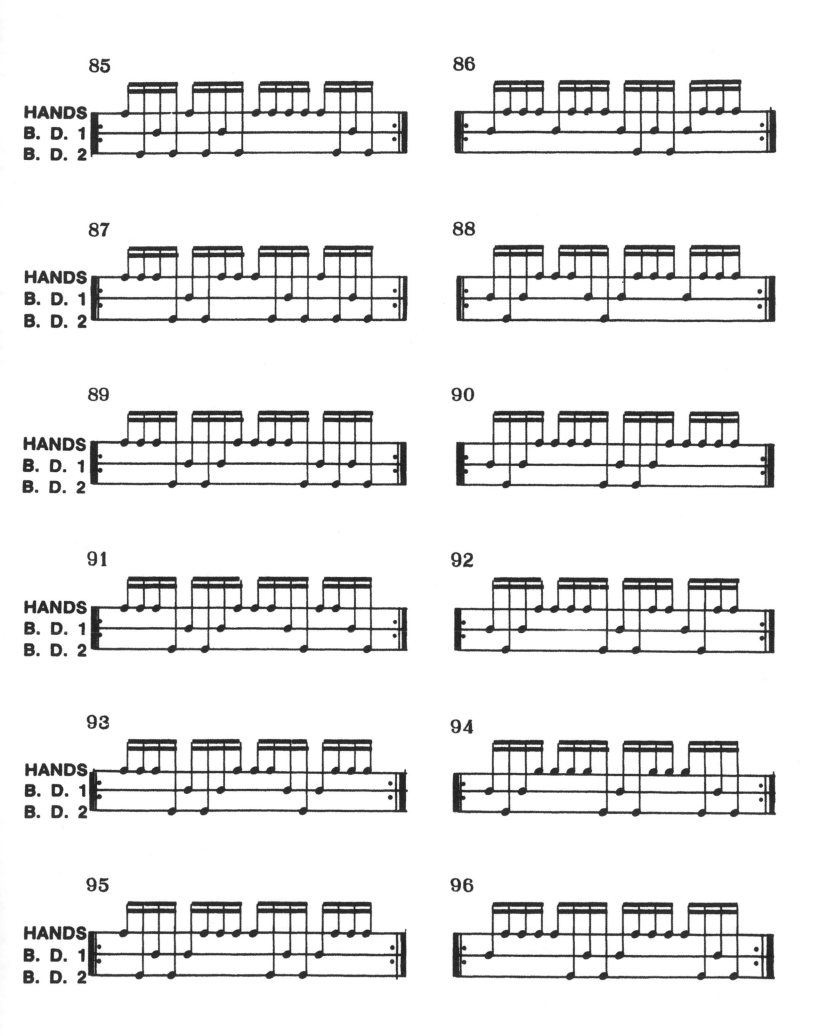

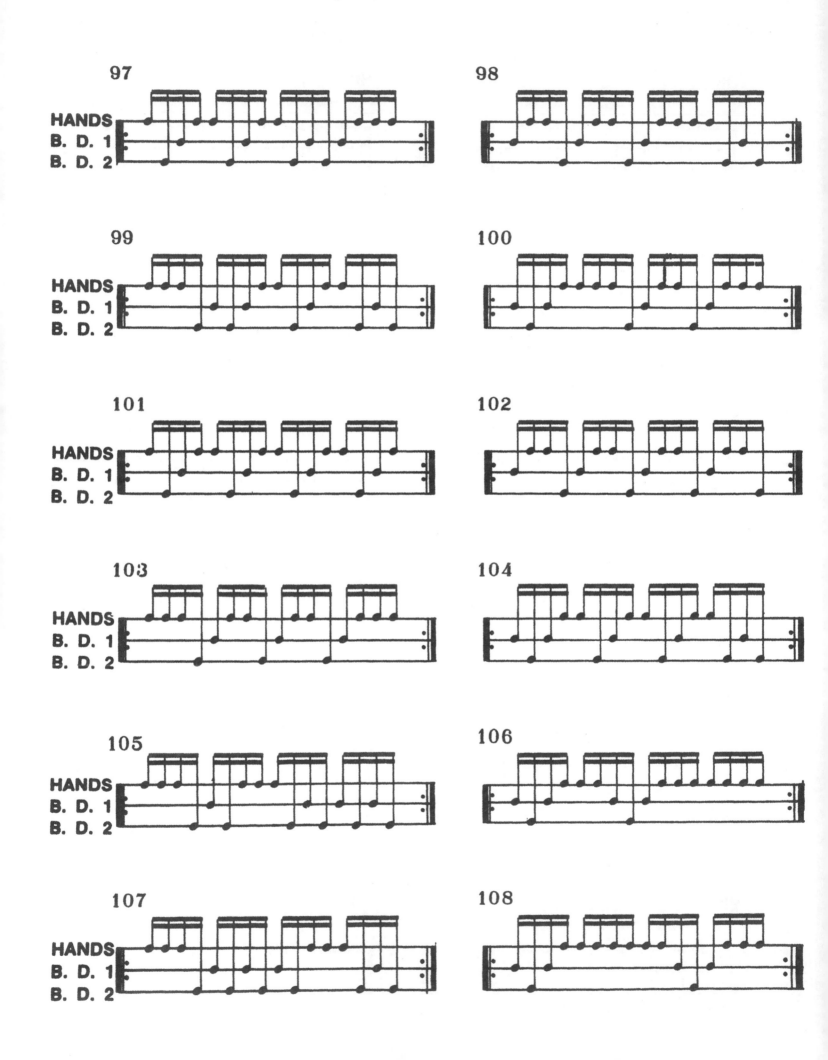

PART IIB   EIGHTH NOTE TRIPLET FILLS

In this section fills are formed by breaking up continuous eighth note triplets between both hands and both feet When playing these fills, use the Single Stroke System for both your hands and feet That is, start with your lead hand or foot and then alternate strokes Here is the key to playing these fills.

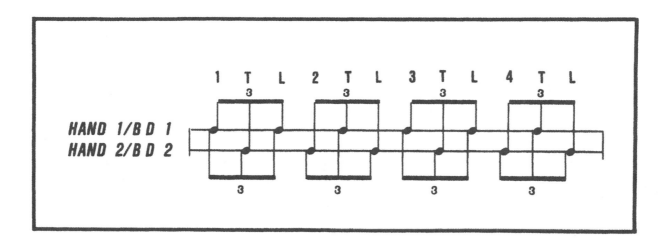

By using this system your lead hand and foot will fall on the "1" of the measure following the fill For example, for a right-handed player·

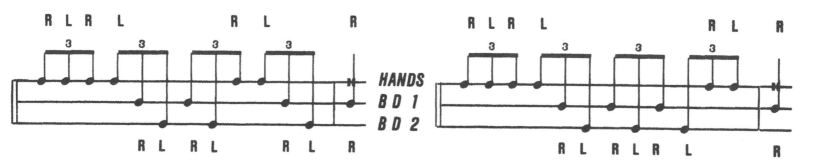

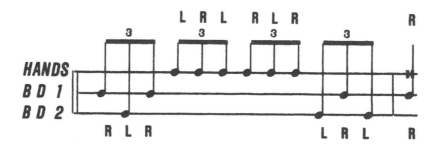

Practice playing these fills with a shuffle beat similar to

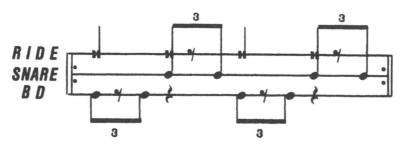

or any beat in Part IB

43

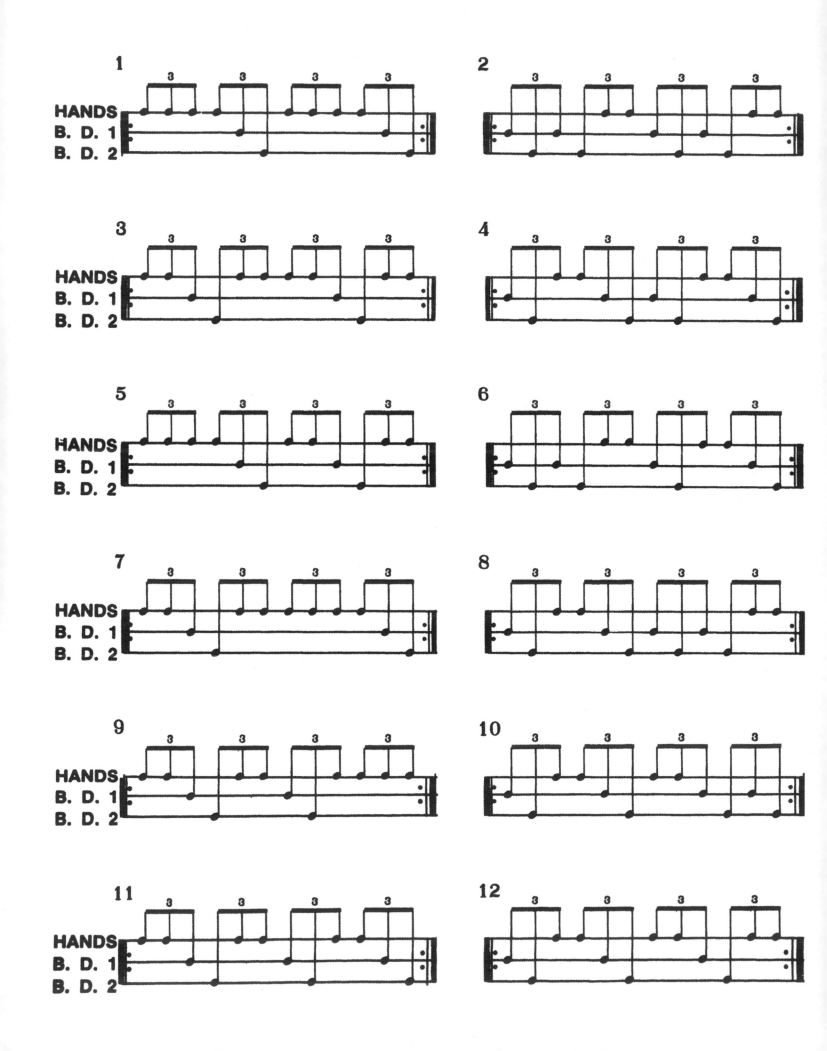

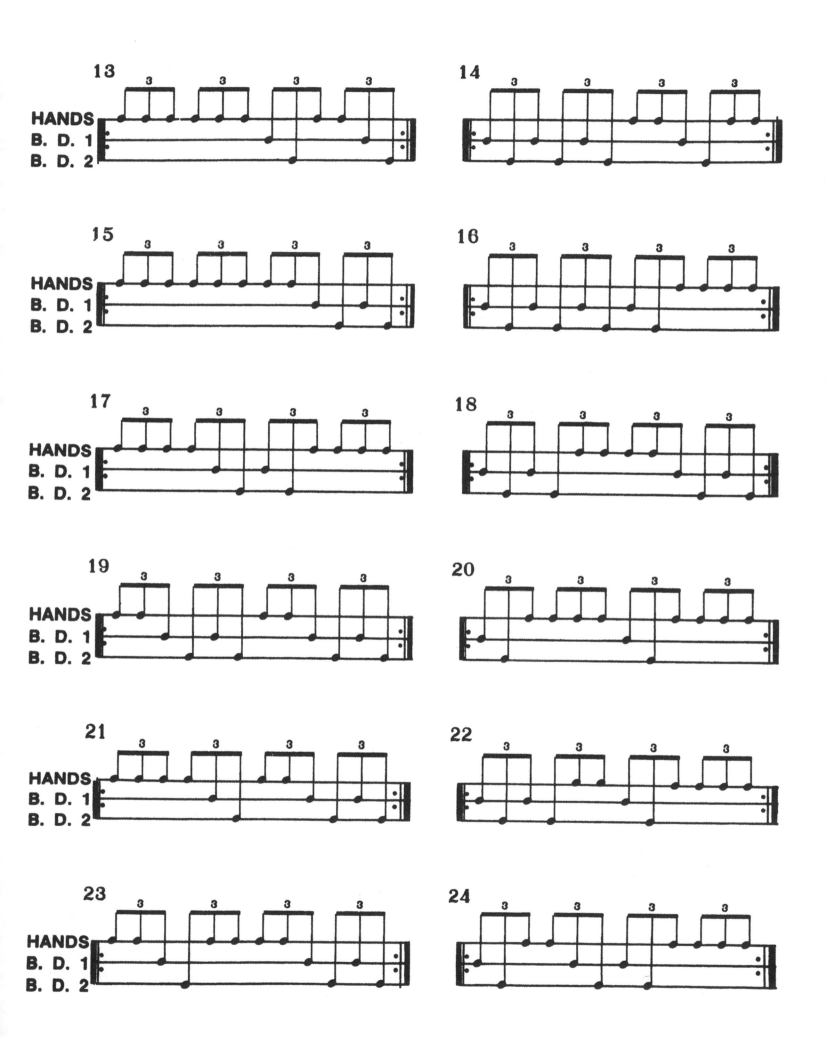

45

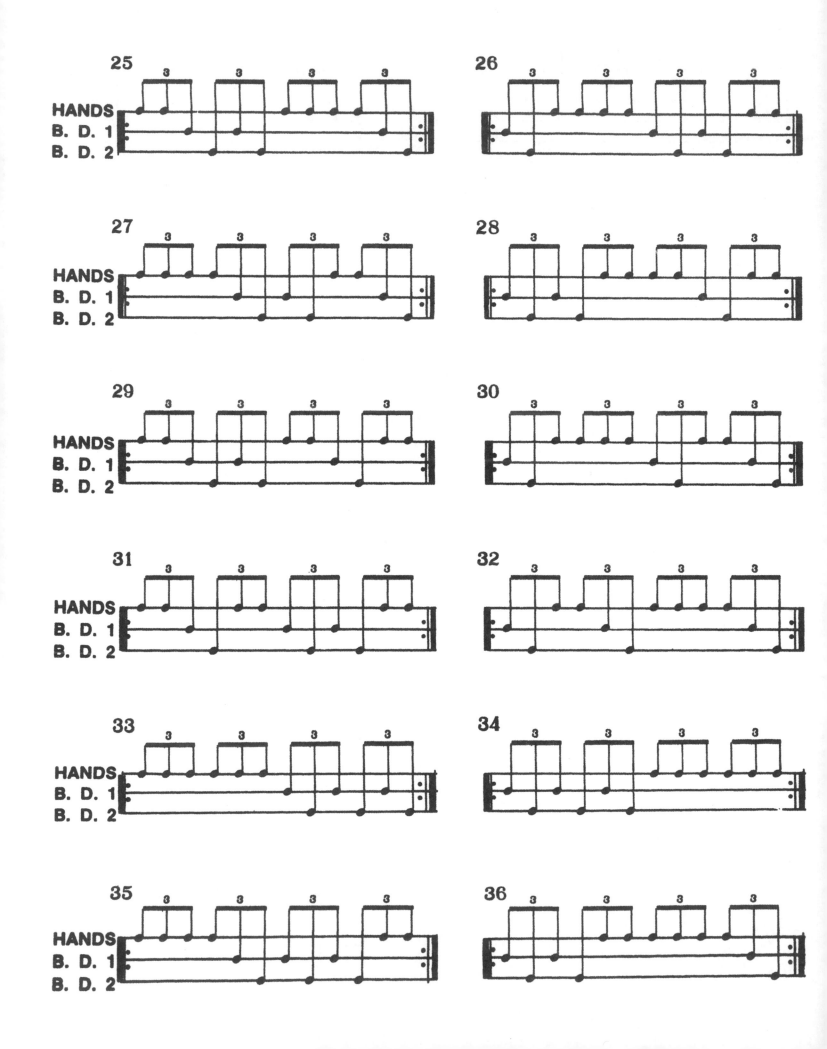

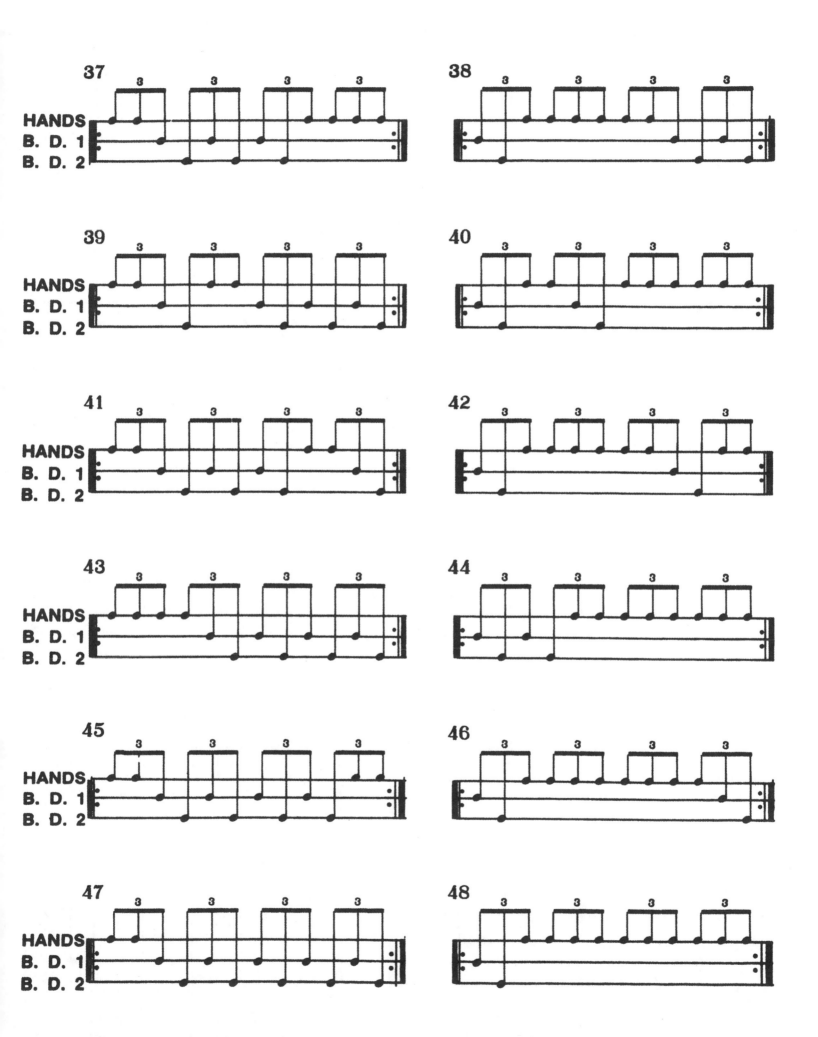

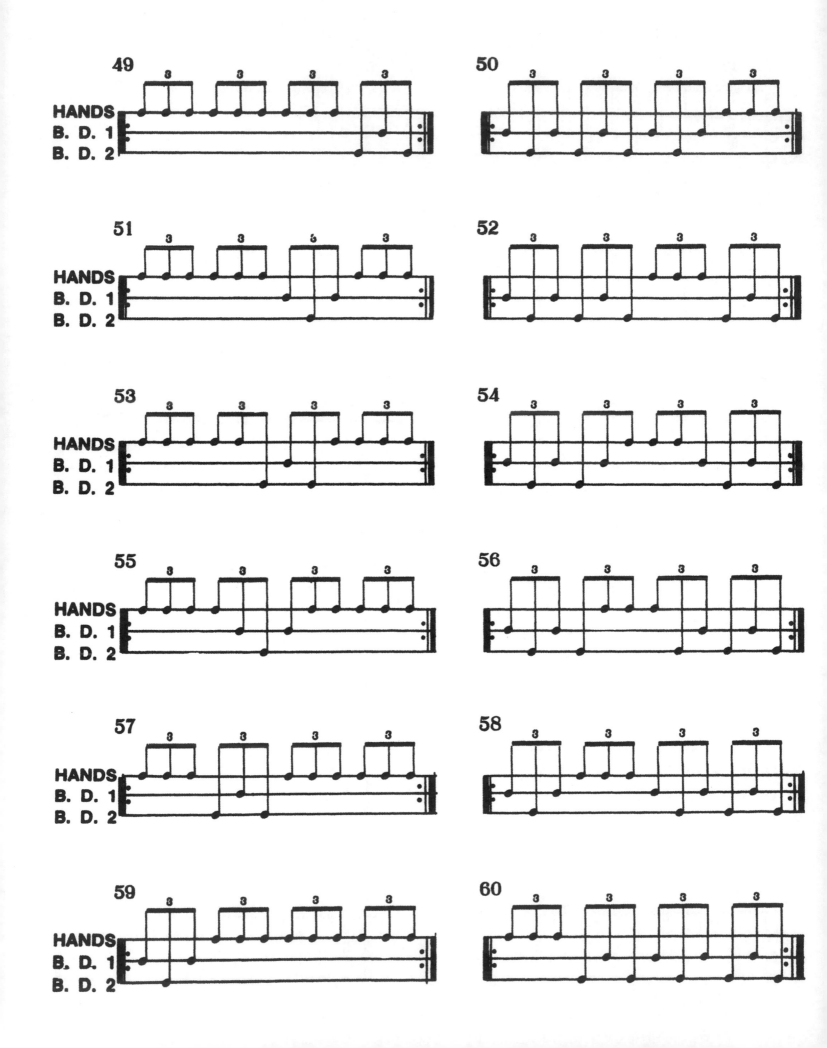

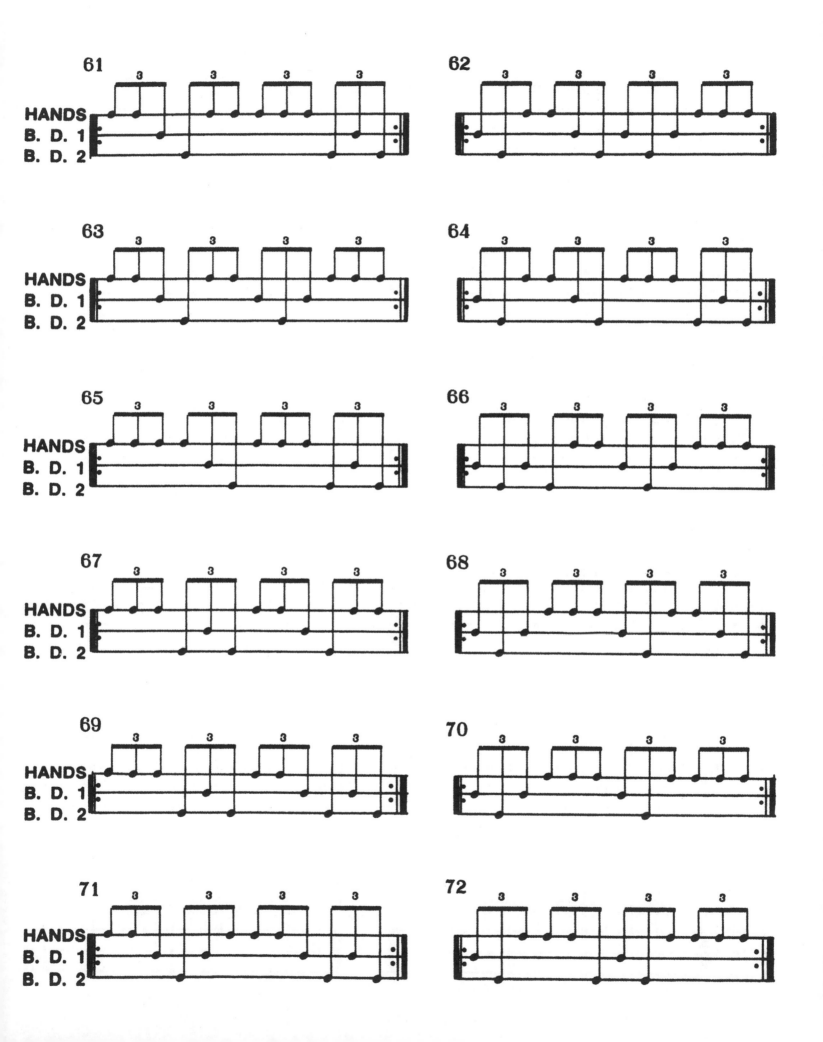

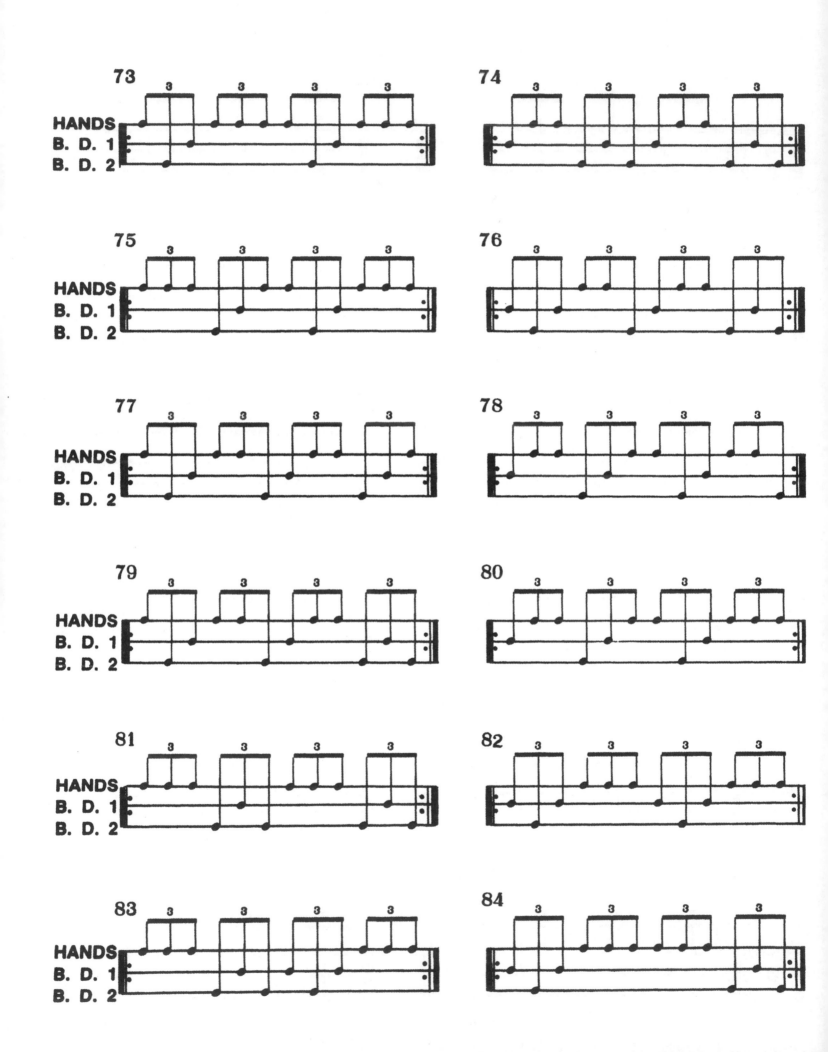

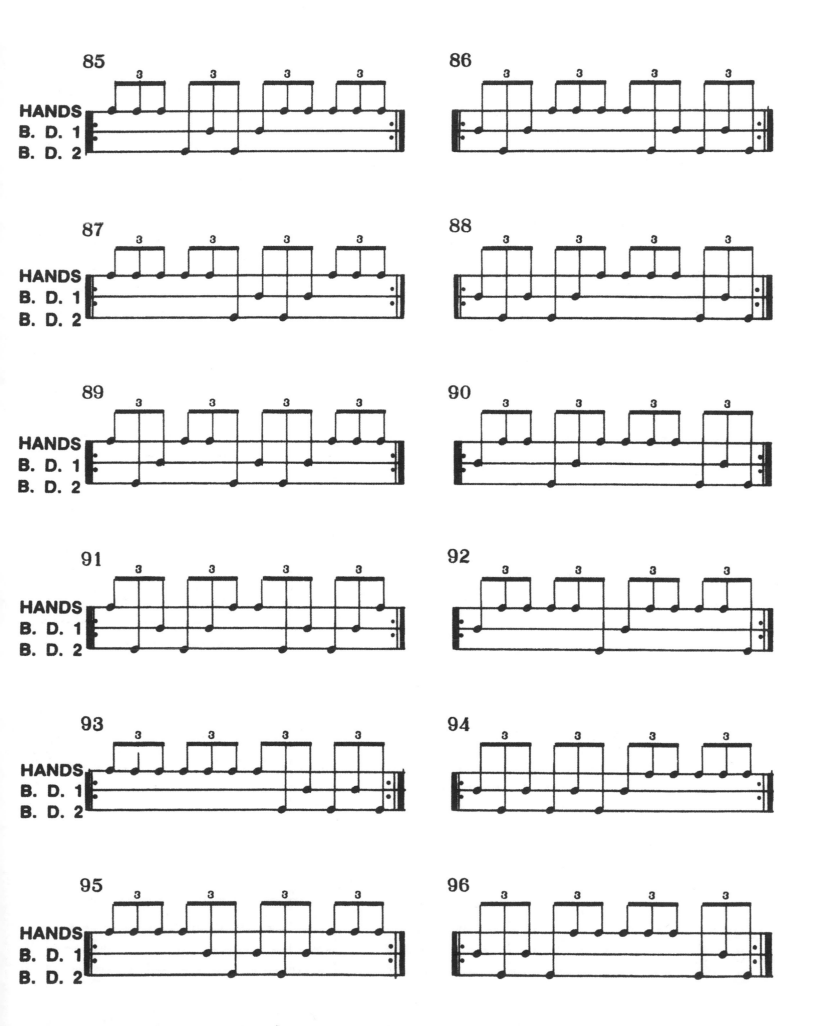

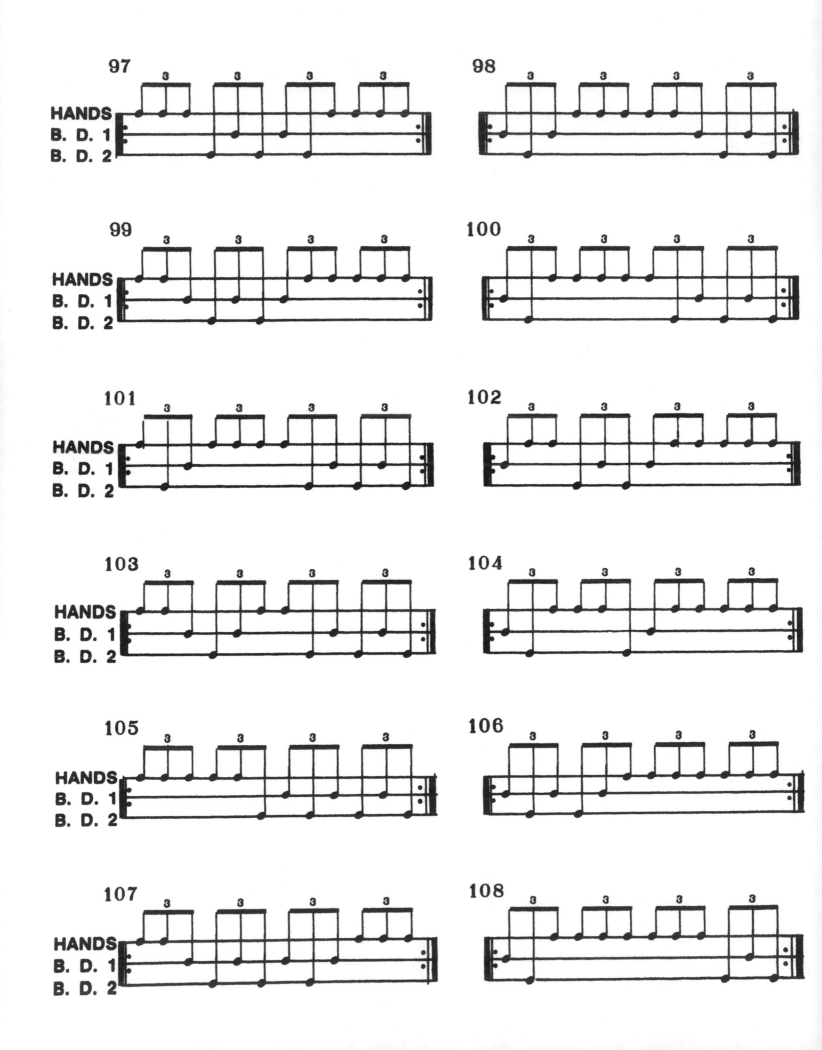

Broken Fill Patterns

All of the fill patterns of Part II consisted of *continuous* sixteenth notes or eighth note triplets. The same system can be used when playing *non-continuous* or *broken* fill patterns between both hands and both feet. Experiment with different rhythmic patterns. Here are some examples:

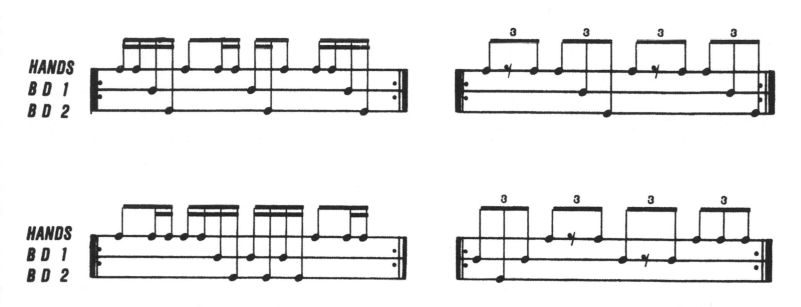

Echoing The Hands With The Feet

Another concept that can be used in playing fills or in soloing is echoing the hands with the feet In the following examples the second half of the measure echoes the first half·

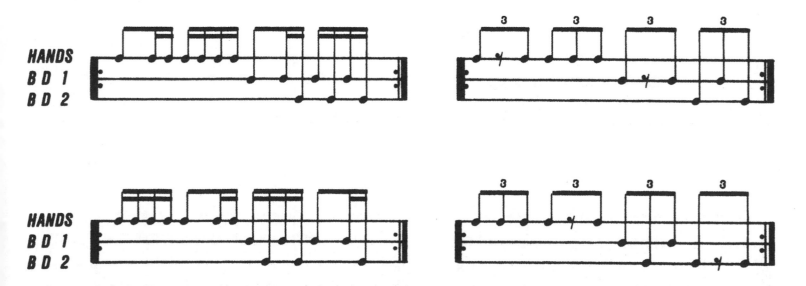

Try expanding on this concept by echoing 1, 2, 4 or motre measures.

<u>Overlapping Patterns</u>

The following patterns overlap hands and feet Try using this concept in your fills and solos

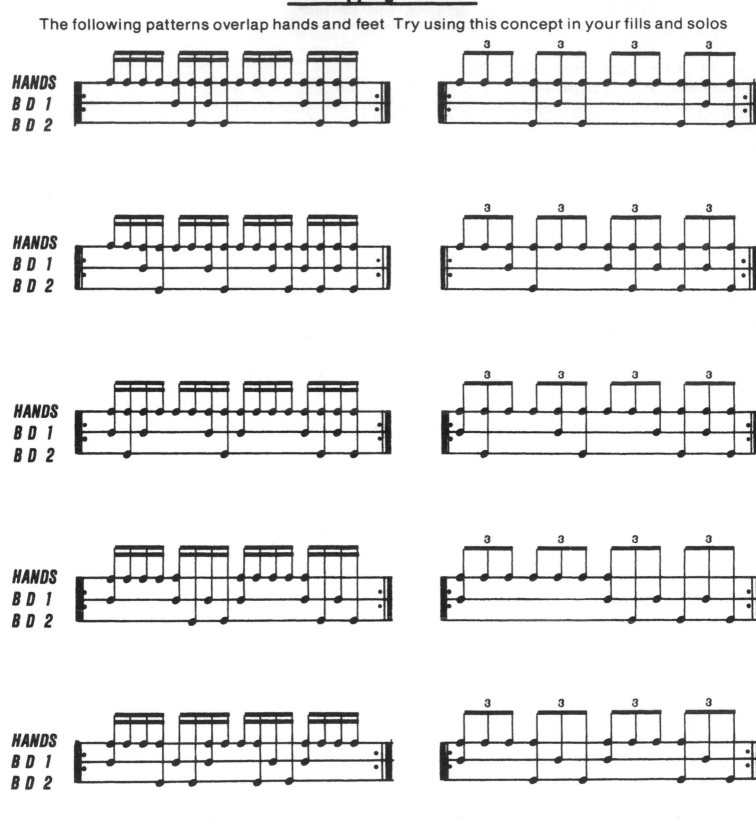

PART III   SOLOING OVER THE DOUBLE BASS ROLL

In Part III various hand patterns are played over the double bass drum roll.* These patterns include Accented Rolls and their Accent Patterns, and Mixed Sticking Patterns. Part IIIA deals with the sixteenth note feel and Part IIIB with the triplet feel This part of the book is designed to:
- Present different hand patterns that are useful in soloing
- Develop hand independence over the double bass roll
- Develop balance, control and stamina on double bass

When practicing Part III, first become familiar with each hand pattern Repeat each pattern on the snare over the double bass roll until you are comfortable with it before moving on to the next. Keep in mind, when rolling with your hands and feet simultaneously, you should not hear flamming Once you are comfortable with the patterns, move them around the drums. Play them into each other as solos of 4, 8, 16 or more measures. Playing these hand patterns as extended solos over the double bass roll will increase your stamina on double bass.

PARTS III — A1, B1   ACCENTED ROLLS AND ACCENT PATTERNS

In Parts III A1 and B1, an Accented (single stroke) Roll (left column of each page) and the Accent (or syncopated) Pattern of that roll (right column of each page) are played over the double bass roll Accented Rolls and Accent Patterns can be interpreted in many ways. Here are a few suggestions for playing this section
- Play the accented roll on the snare using rimshots for all accents.
- Play the accented roll on any one drum by playing the accents loud and the unaccented (ghost) notes soft
- Play all the accents on toms and other parts of the kit while playing the unaccented notes on the snare
- After playing the Accented Rolls, play only the Accent Pattern (right column of each page) Break up the patterns between both hands Try using the Single Stroke System for sticking (as in Part II) or experiment with other sticking methods. Keep in mind that playing the Accent Pattern over the double bass roll is not as easy as playing the continuous Accented Roll This will serve as a good balance and control exercise
- Play the Accent Patterns with both hands simultaneously
- To further develop your hand independence over the double bass roll, try playing the Accent Pattrns on the snare with one hand, while playing one of the following Ride Patterns with the other.

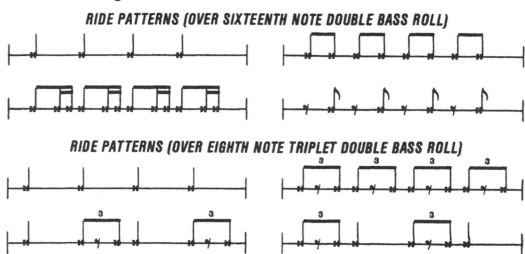

*NOTE: The double bass roll is written only once on each page (at the bottom); however EVERY hand pattern should be played over the double bass roll.

PART III A2, B2   MIXED STICKING PATTERNS

In Parts III A2 and B2, Mixed Sticking Patterns are played over the double bass roll These patterns can be used in soloing as well as in creating counter rhythms and fills. The patterns are written as R (right hand) and L (left hand). Every pattern is paired with its "mirror-image" in which R=L and L=R. It is important to play both

All of these patterns are composed of combinations of single and double strokes All of the fundamental sticking patterns are included the single and double stroke roll, the single, double and triple paradiddle; the paradiddle-diddle, and many inversions of each Since there are not more than two consecutive strokes with one hand, they should be able to be played with a constant flow.

Besides practical applications, these patterns are helpful in developing hand independence over the feet You will be playing different combinations of hands and feet together When working out these patterns, it may be helpful to play them on two different surfaces so you can hear the rhythm that each hand is playing Keep in mind that these patterns are written without accents. Experiment with some of your own accents

Besides using these patterns in soloing, try using them to form beats by playing R and L on the RIDE and SNARE For example.

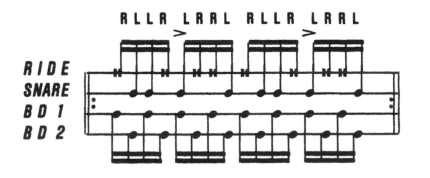

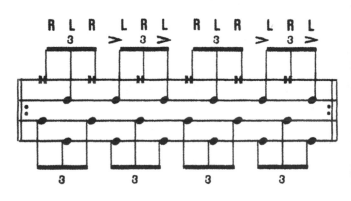

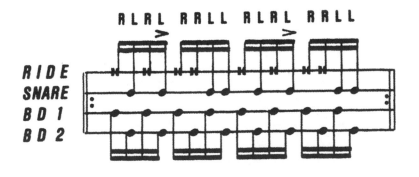

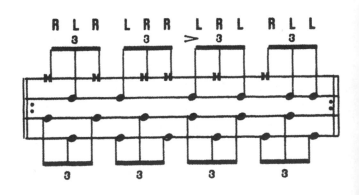

Part III A1
ACCENTED SIXTEENTH NOTES

56

Accented Roll　　　　　　　　　　**Accent Pattern**

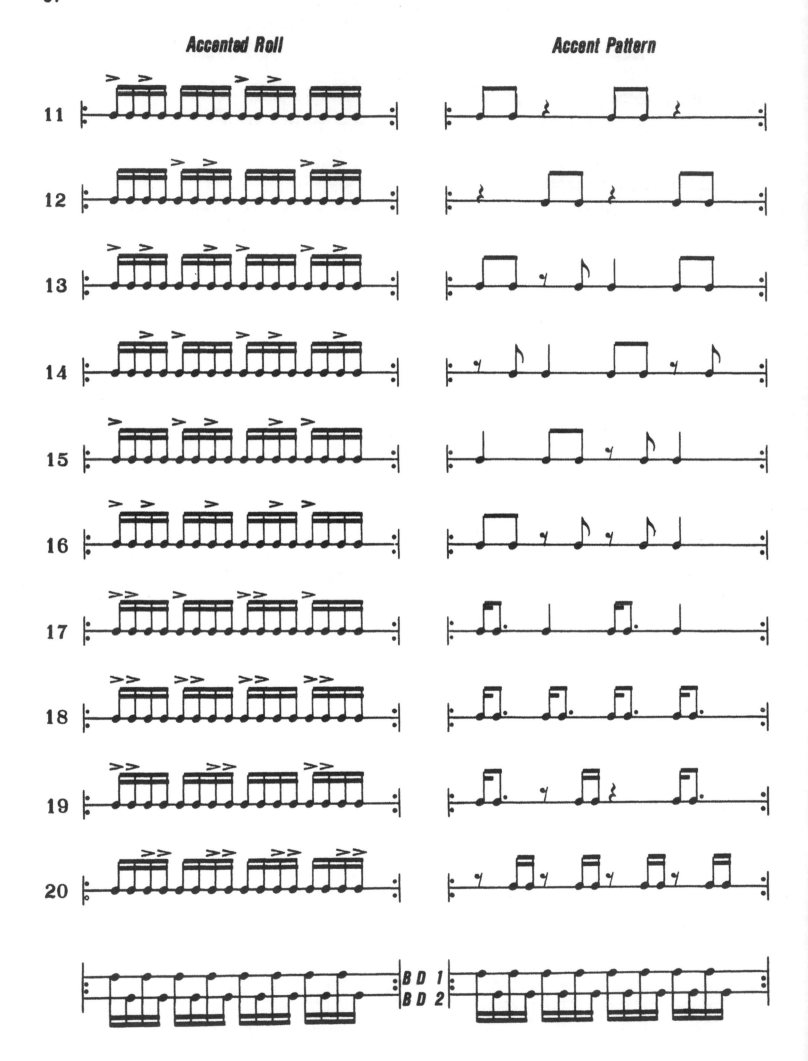

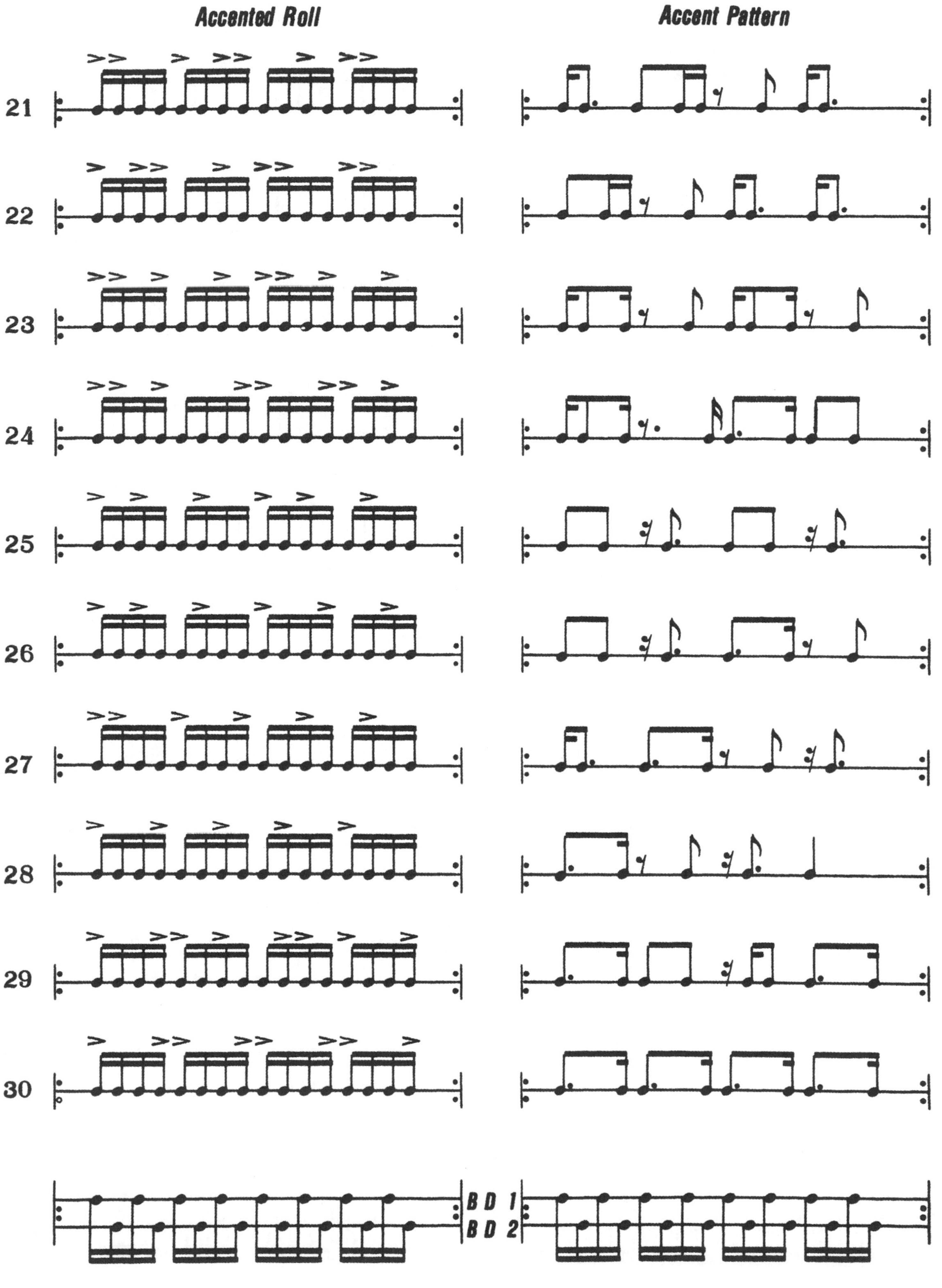
Accented Roll
Accent Pattern
21
22
23
24
25
26
27
28
29
30
B D 1
B D 2

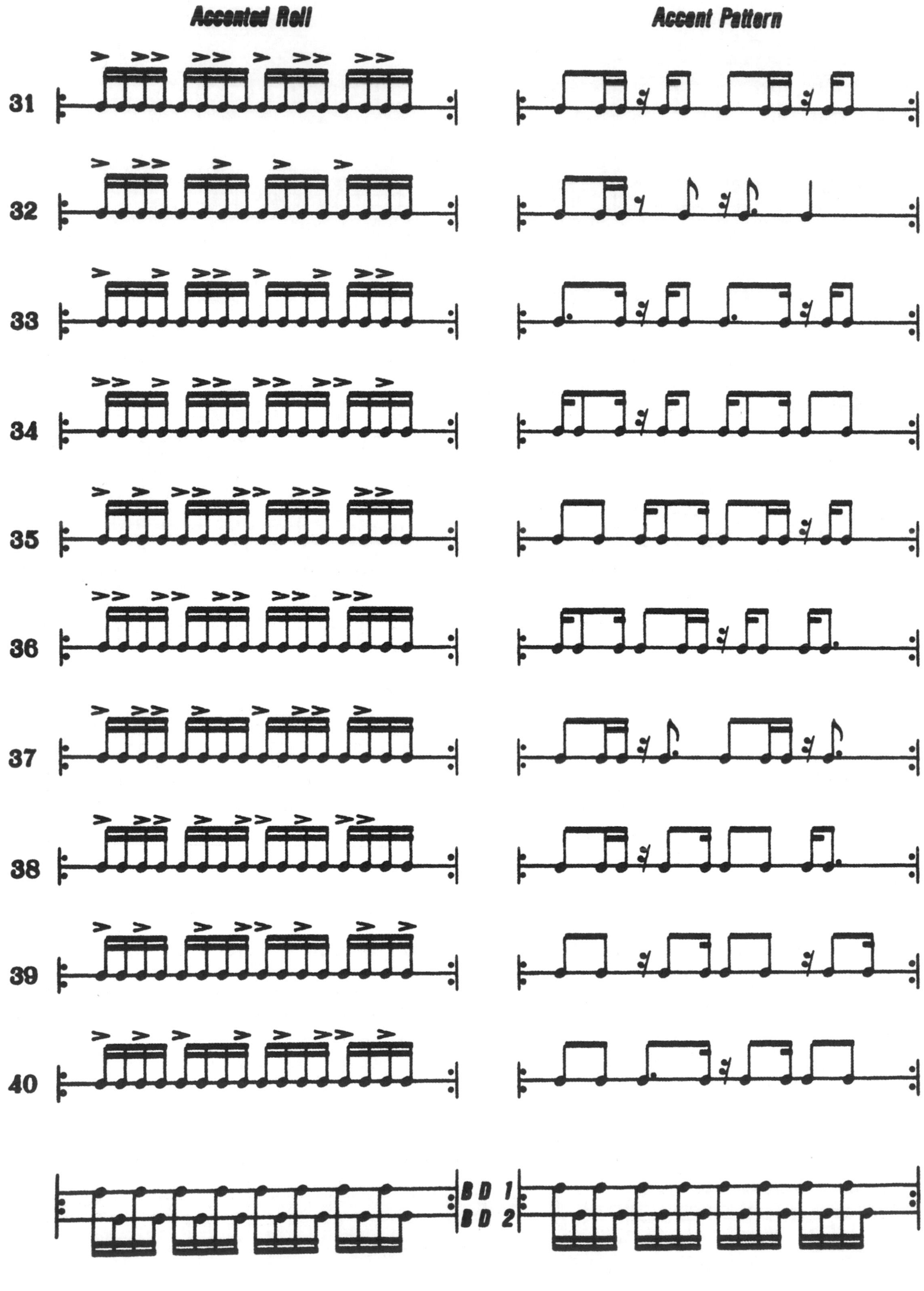
Accented Roll
Accent Pattern
31
32
33
34
35
36
37
38
39
40
B D 1
B D 2

Accented Roll — Accent Pattern

PART III A2
SIXTEENTH NOTES WITH MIXED STICKING

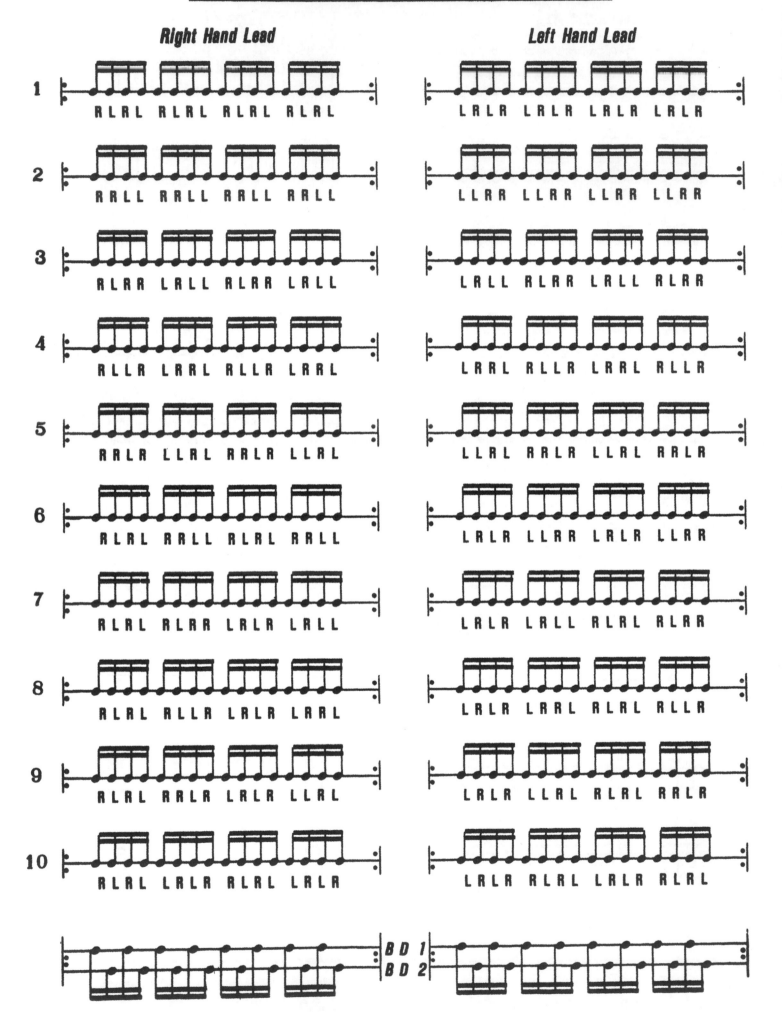

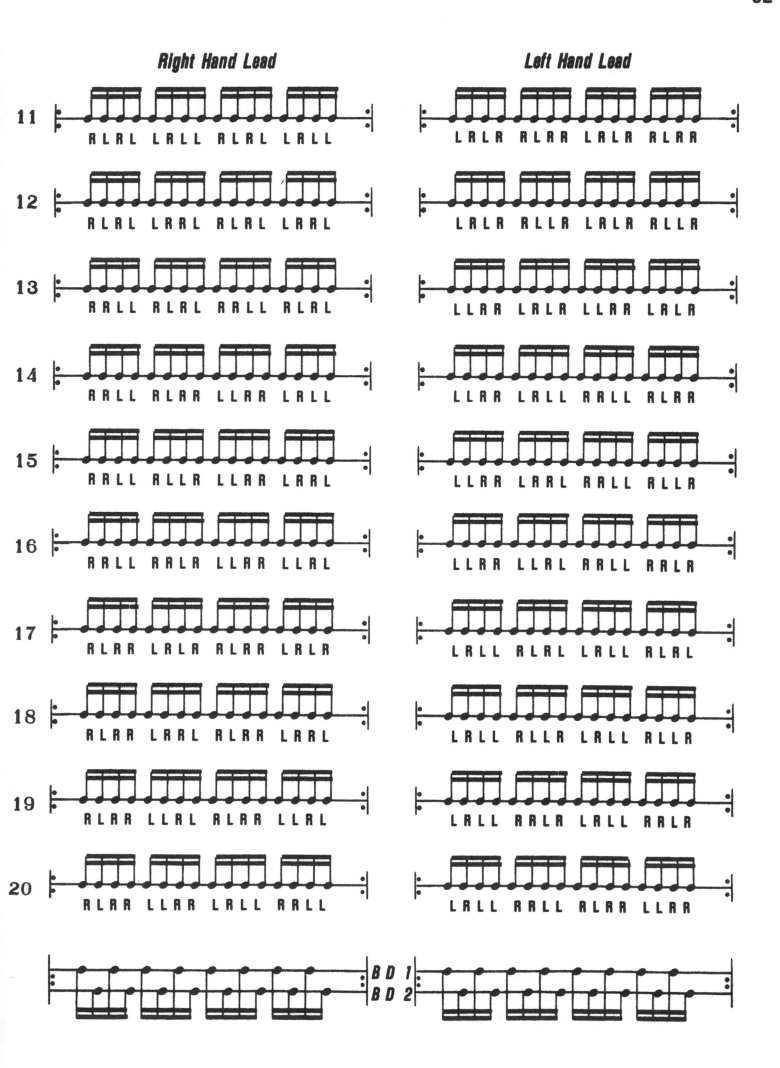

63

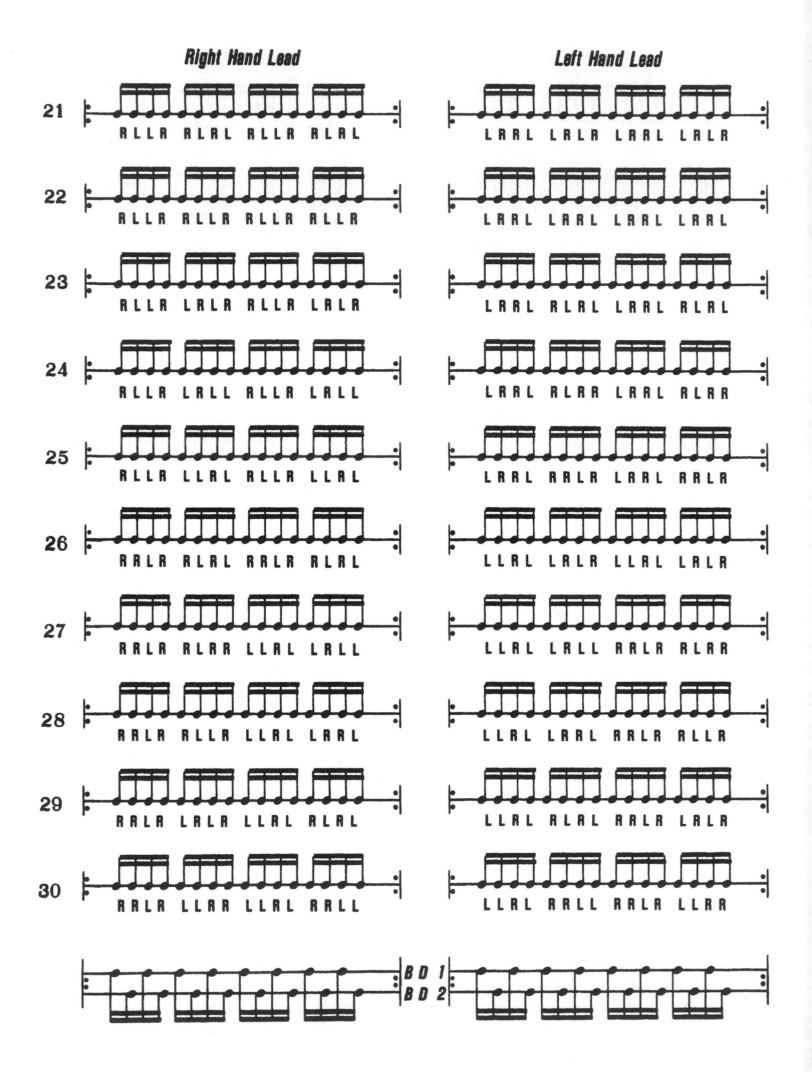

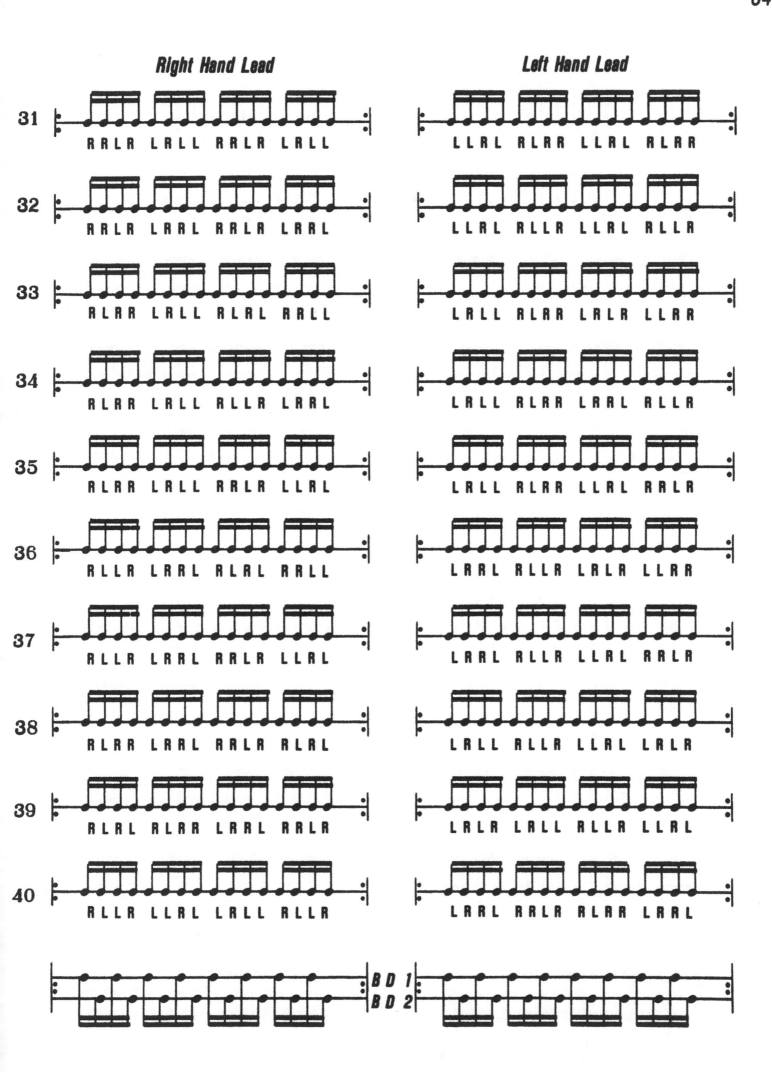

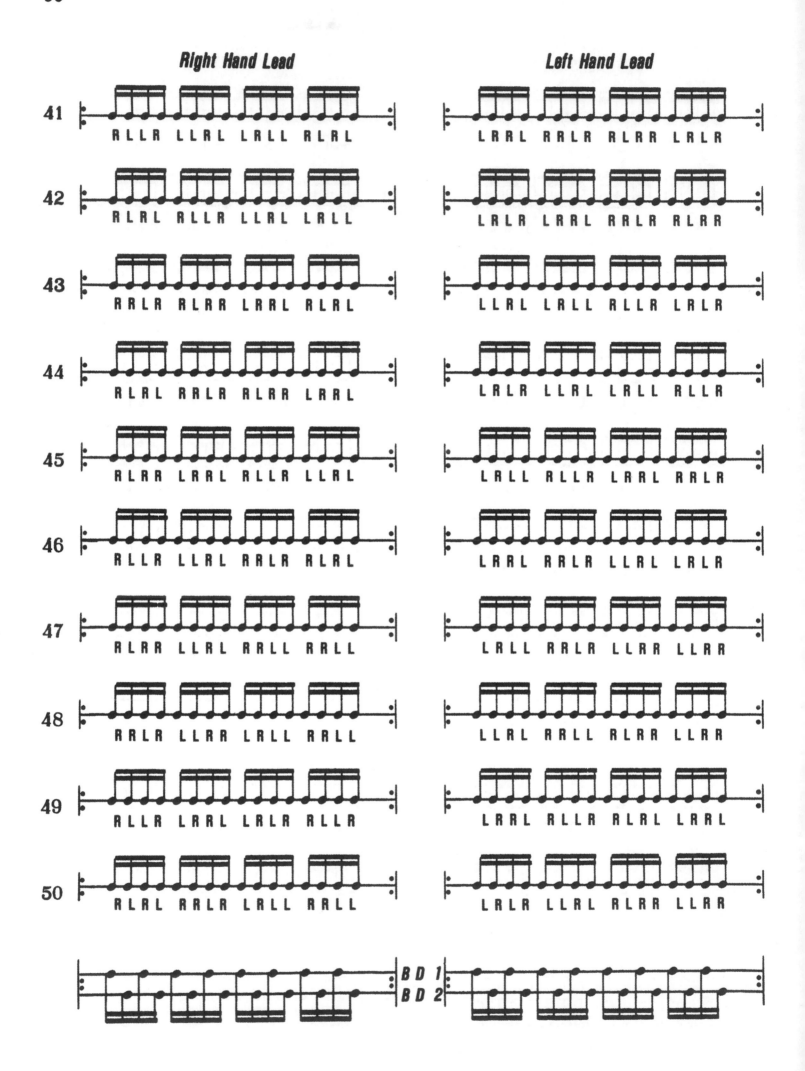

Accented Roll

Accent Pattern

67

Accented Roll   **Accent Pattern**

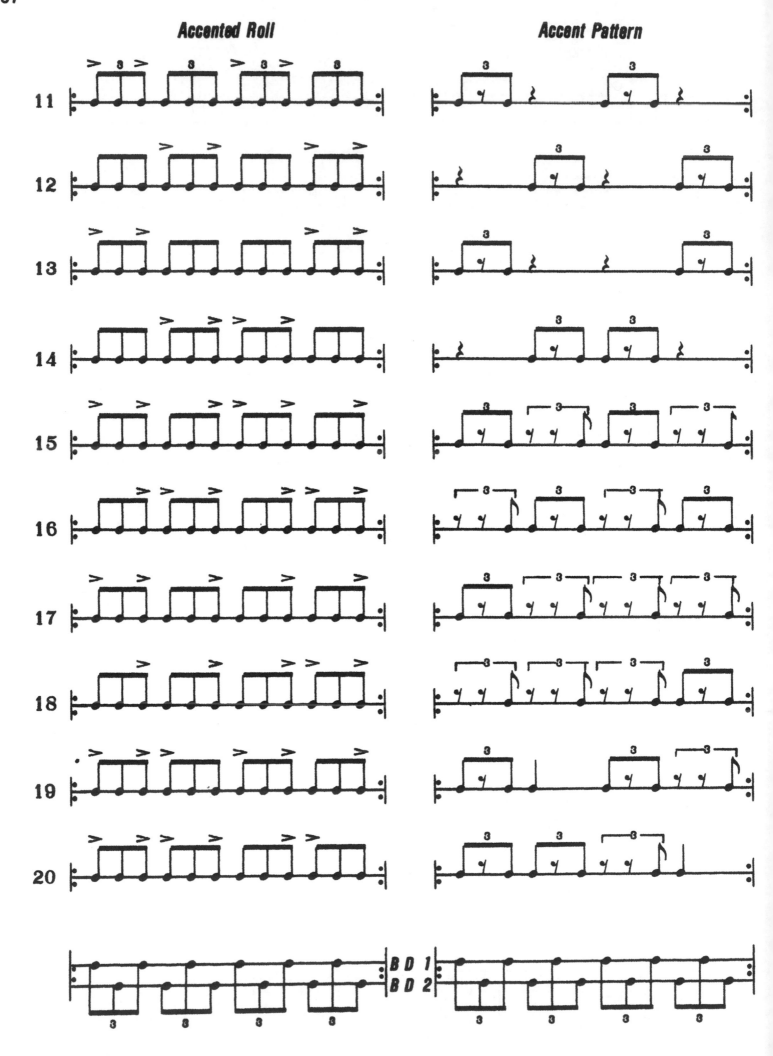

68

Accented Roll　　　　　　　　Accent Pattern

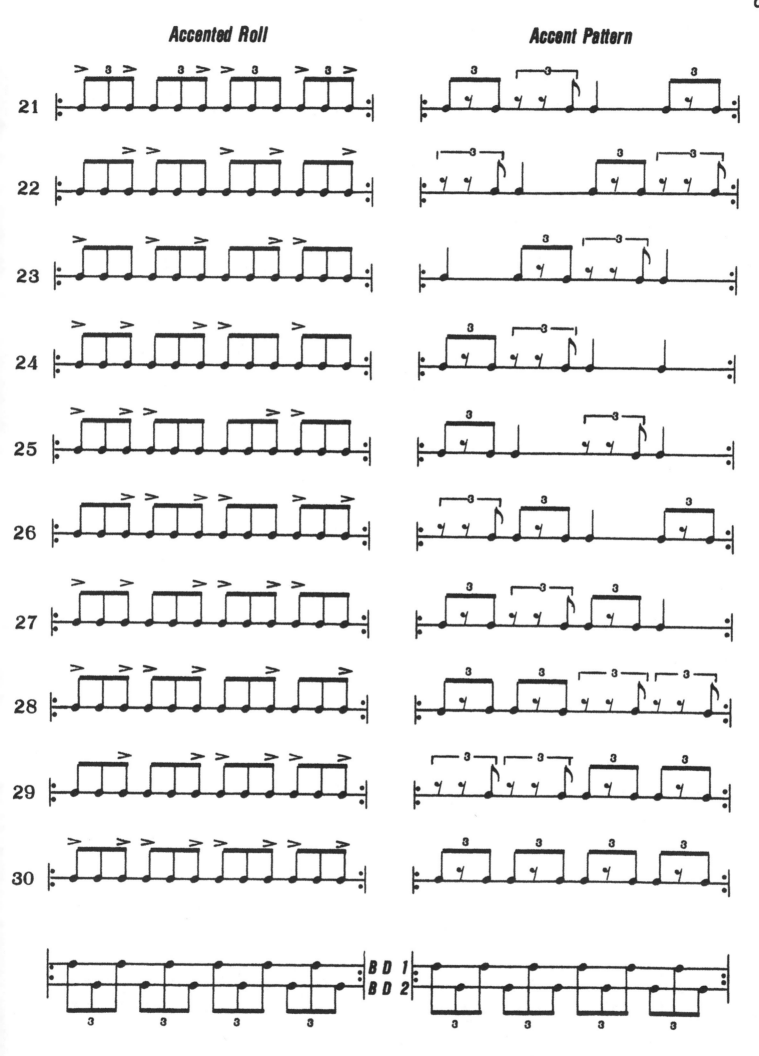

Accented Roll

Accent Pattern

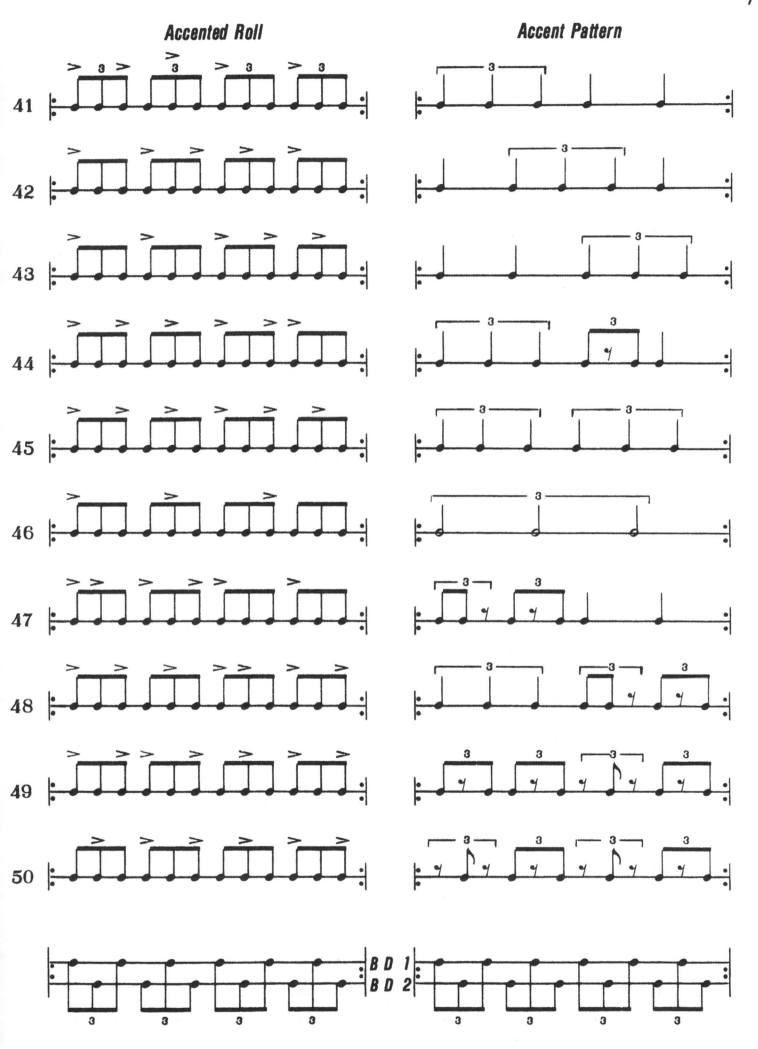

Part III B2
TRIPLETS WITH MIXED STICKING

Right Hand Lead   **Left Hand Lead**

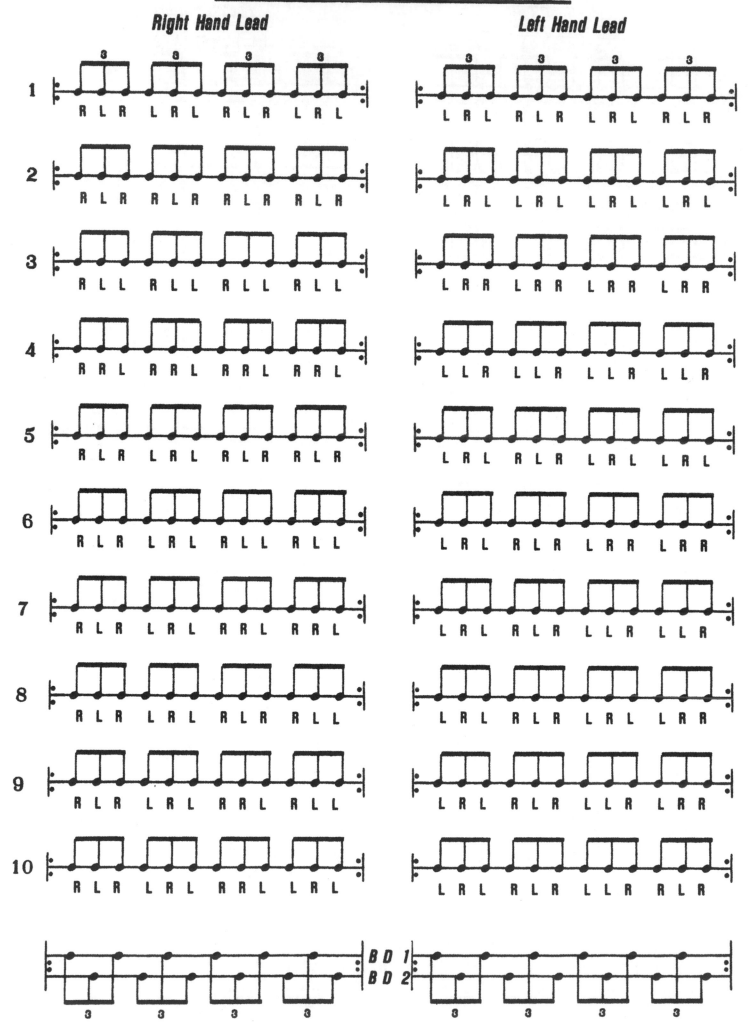

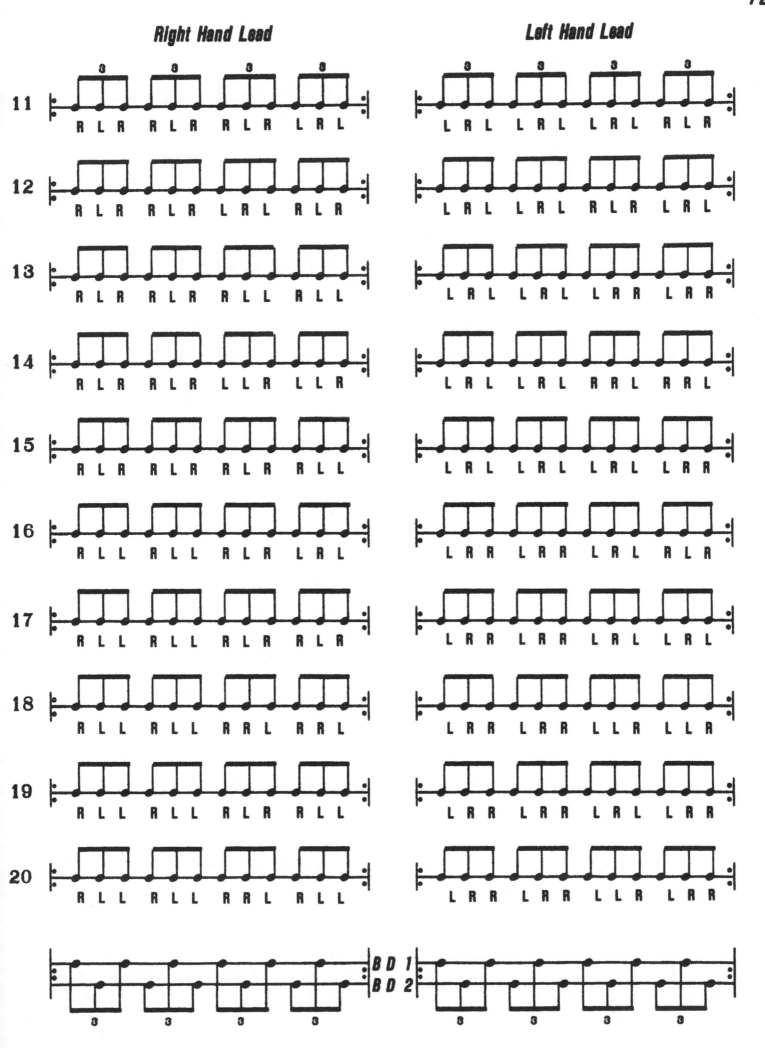

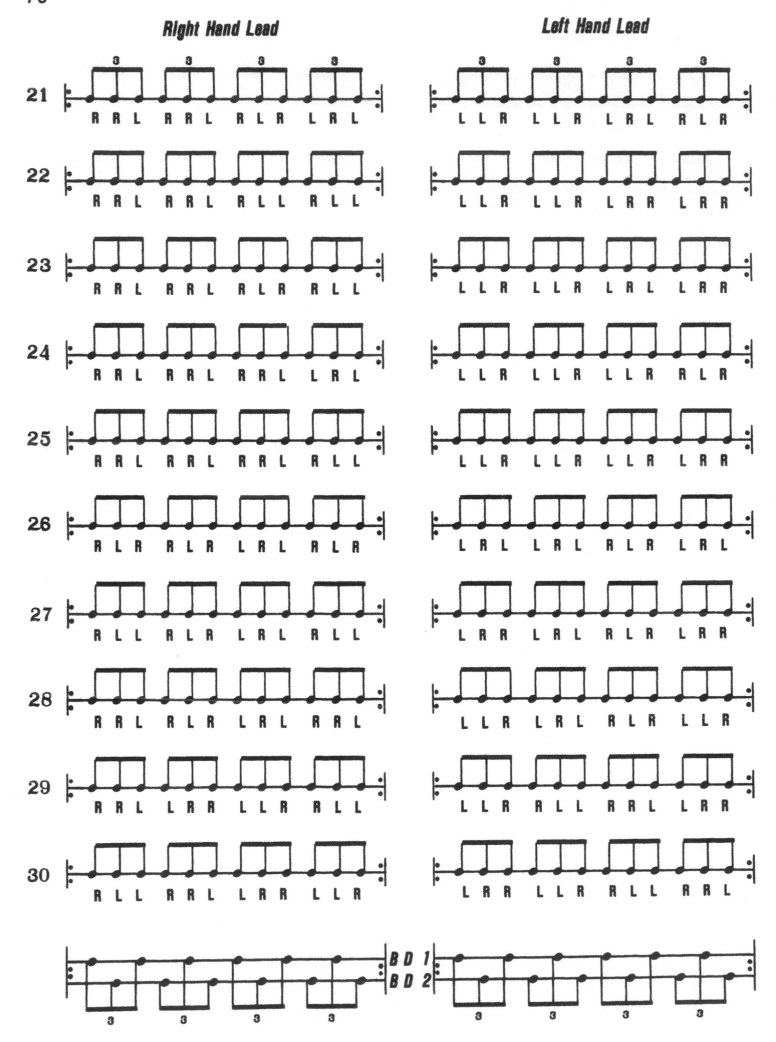

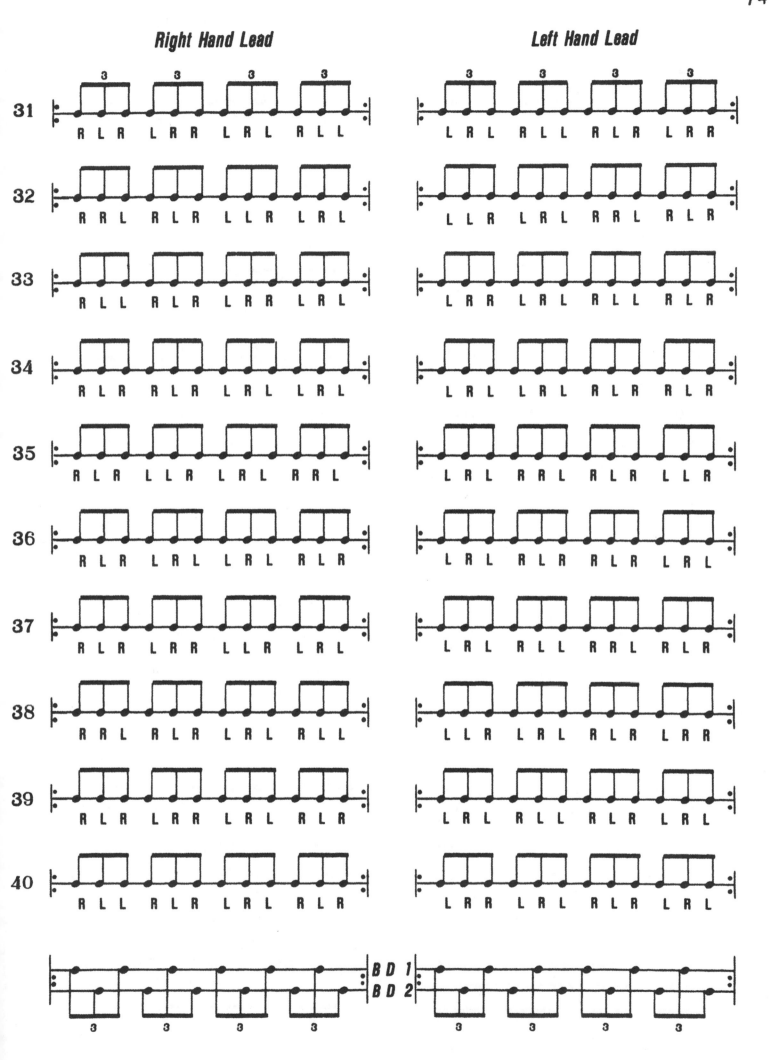

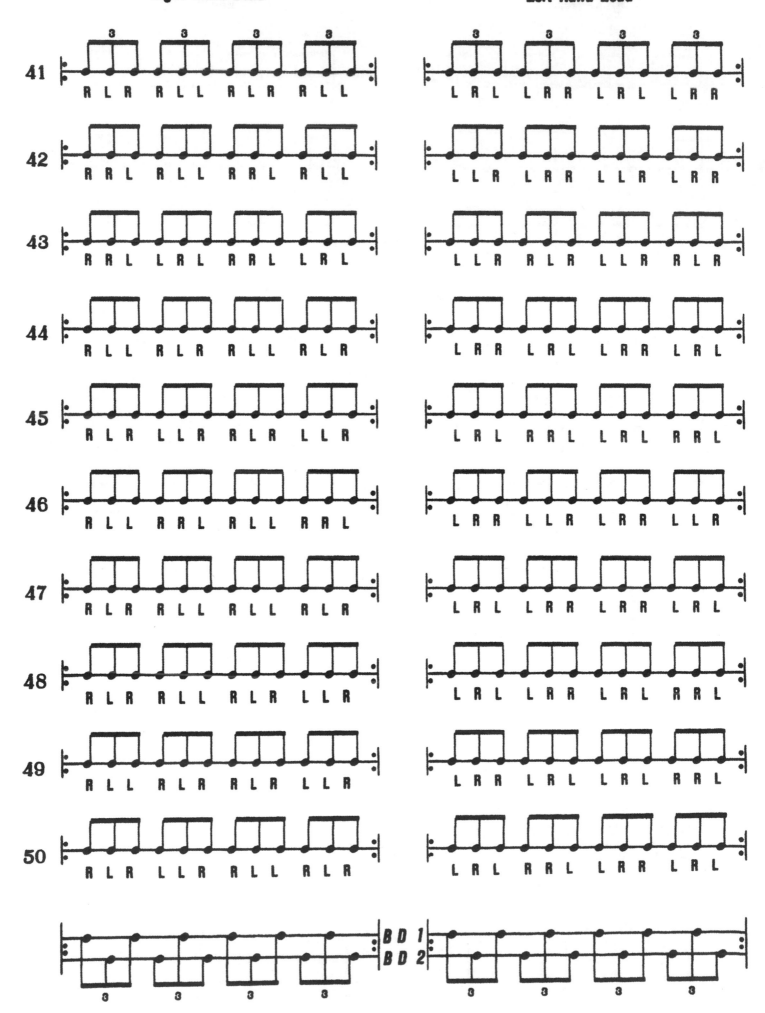

Soloing over Broken Bass Drum Patterns

Once Part III has been mastered as written, try playing the same hand patterns over different bass drum patterns. Try using some of the bass drum patterns in Part I. Here are a few examples:

Sixteenth Note Bass Drum Patterns

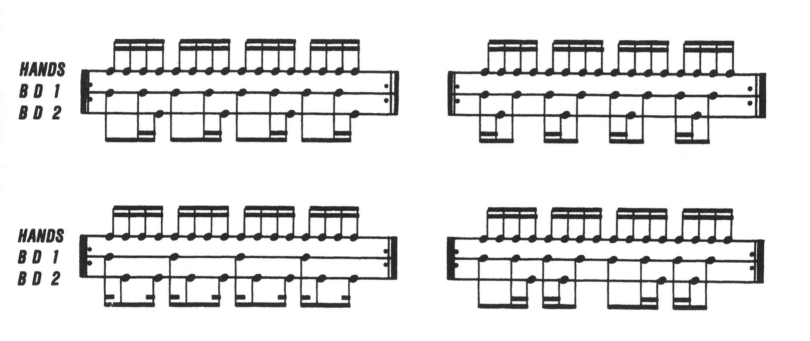

Eighth Note Triplet Bass Drum Patterns

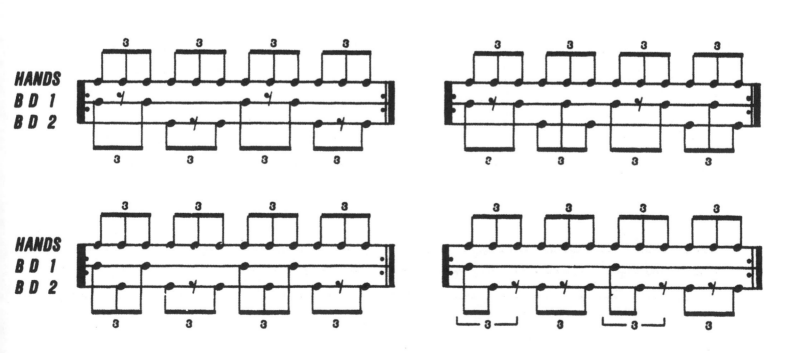